EARLY YEARS
AROUND THE YEAR

Communication, language and literacy
Seasonal activities

Lorraine Gale

Seasonal ideas • Festival activities • Early learning goals

CREDITS

British Library Cataloguing-in-Publication Data
A catalogue record for this book is available from the British Library.

ISBN 0 439 01821 8

AUTHOR
Lorraine Gale

EDITOR
Lesley Sudlow

ASSISTANT EDITOR
Saveria Mezzana

SERIES DESIGNER
Anna Oliwa

DESIGNER
Narinder Sandhu

ILLUSTRATIONS
Jenny Tulip

COVER ILLUSTRATION
Anna Hopkins

ACKNOWLEDGEMENTS
The publishers gratefully acknowledge permission to reproduce the following copyright material:

Ann Bryant for 'Summer sun shines on and on' by Ann Bryant © 2001 Ann Bryant, previously unpublished; **Celia Warren** for 'A piplock teaser', 'Sing a song of spligworth', 'Minifeasts for minibeasts' and 'Five little woodlice' by Celia Warren © 2001 Celia Warren, all previously unpublished.

Text © 2001 Lorraine Gale
© 2001 Scholastic Ltd

Published by Scholastic Ltd, Villiers House, Clarendon Avenue, Leamington Spa, Warwickshire CV32 5PR

Designed using Adobe Pagemaker
Printed by Proost NV, Belgium

Visit our website at www.scholastic.co.uk

1 2 3 4 5 6 7 8 9 0   1 2 3 4 5 6 7 8 9 0

CONTENTS

Around the year

The aims of this series

This book forms part of a series of six books that provide practical activities to support the Early Learning Goals (QCA). Each book focuses on a different area of learning. As the title of the series suggests, the books can be used throughout the year, with activities and ideas for each of the four seasons and the multicultural festivals and special days that fall within them. Early years practitioners will find the activities an invaluable source of new ideas that can be dipped into at any time of the year.

Communication, language and literacy

The main aim of this book is to provide a variety of easy-to-follow activities to help young children to become competent speakers, listeners, readers and writers. It draws on a range of seasonal opportunities and multicultural festivals for its inspiration. Festivals are included from each of the major religions. Although not every festival for each religion is covered in this book, a selection of the most important ones are included, such as Wesak, Christmas and Pesach. There are also some activities dedicated to less well-known festivals such as Kodomono-hi and Ganjitsu. A brief description of each festival covered and the date that they are celebrated has been provided on pages 7 and 8.

About the book

This book is divided into four chapters. Each chapter focuses on one season of the year – Spring, Summer, Autumn and Winter. Each chapter contains fourteen activities with a range of learning objectives linked to the Early Learning Goals (QCA) to help children to develop their communication and language skills. The ideas suggested can be applied equally well to the

documents on pre-school education published for Scotland, Wales and Northern Ireland. Six activities for each chapter are based around seasonal events and happenings such as new growth, leaves falling or spring-cleaning. The remaining eight activities of each chapter focus on seasonal festivals and celebrations.

How to use this book

Each activity follows the same format starting with a 'Learning objective' that outlines the key skills, knowledge, concepts or attitudes that the children will be developing. 'Group size' is given for each activity; however, these are only guidelines and you should change these as necessary to suit your own setting. 'Small' groups are those with between four and six children in them. Activities labelled for 'large' groups are best for groups with at least ten children, although they could be adapted for smaller groups.

The 'What you need' section lists the resources required to carry out the

activity. Most resources mentioned should be readily available in any early years setting. Some of the activities require the children to listen to a relevant story, some of which are included on the photocopiable sheets. Recommended book titles can usually be borrowed or ordered from a library. Alternatively, you may prefer to use a

similar book of your own. Computers and software have only been used as optional resources to ensure that all the activities can be used by anyone in any early years setting.

Where an activity involves cooking or handling of food, this symbol (!) will remind you to check for any allergies and dietary requirements.

The 'What to do' section provides step-by-step instructions on how to carry out each activity. Throughout the book, the emphasis is on using a 'hands-on' approach that builds on the children's current knowledge and prior experiences.

Although the activities are aimed at four-year-olds, the 'Support' section gives suggestions about how the main activity can be adapted for younger children or those with special needs, and the 'Extension' section explains how the main activity can be extended for older or more able children.

The book includes 16 photocopiable sheets that are used to support some of the activities and there is a range of stories, poems and templates on these pages that may be copied. Guidelines on how many copies of each sheet are needed are included in the 'What you need' or 'Preparation' sections.

Links with home

Encourage parents and carers to be involved with their children's learning as much as possible. This book suggests simple activities they can carry out at home with them.

Some carers may not be familiar with the festivals covered in the book; others, however, may have first-hand knowledge of the celebrations. Invite them to come and talk to the group about how they celebrate them in their homes, or to help the children to make some traditional food and decorations.

Becoming a competent language user

Give the children as many opportunities as possible to use language by ensuring that books, taped books, a cassette recorder and a selection of paper and writing materials are easily accessible. Make sure you label resources and encourage the children to read and discuss interactive displays.

Choosing books

When selecting books, try to find ones that avoid stereotyping and which show children from other cultures in a positive manner. The text and pictures should be appropriate to the age of the children, their prior experiences and understanding of language.

Festivals

St Patrick's Day (17 March)
An Irish celebration of their patron saint during which people wear shamrocks.

Mother's Day (March/April)
Once a holiday for servant girls to visit their mothers with gifts, it is now a time to show love and appreciation to mothers.

Holi (March/April)
This Hindu festival remembers Prahlada who refused to worship the king regardless of the punishment. Holi traditions today include throwing paint and coloured water over each other.

Easter (March/April)
The most important Christian festival when Jesus' return to life is celebrated. People give chocolate eggs as a symbol of new life.

Pesach/Passover (March/April)
An eight-day Jewish festival commemorating the Jews' exodus from slavery in Egypt. A traditional meal called Seder is eaten.

April Fool's Day (1 April)
Practical jokes are played on other people, but only up until midday. It is possibly a reminder of the date change for New Year in sixteenth-century France from 1 April to 1 January.

Baisakhi (14 April)
The Sikh New Year festival commemorating the five volunteers that offered to sacrifice themselves at Guru Gobind Singh's request.

Kodomono-hi/Japanese Children's Day (5 May)
A Japanese children's festival during which carp-shaped kites are flown, symbolizing strength and determination. Boys bathe with iris leaves to drive away evil and make boys strong.

Wesak (May/June)
Theravada Buddhists celebrate the birth, enlightenment and death of the Buddha on this day. People decorate their temples and homes with candles, flowers and incense.

Shavuot (May/June)
A Jewish festival celebrating the revelation of the Ten Commandments to Moses on Mount Sinai. Synagogues are decorated with flowers and dairy foods.

Midsummer's Day (24 June)
Falls shortly after the longest day of the year. Traditions include bonfires, feasts and torchlit processions.

Father's Day (June)
Children give love and thanks to their fathers during this modern festival.

Dragon Boat Festival (June)
A Chinese festival honouring Ch'u Yuan who drowned himself in protest at the Emperor. Today dragon boat races symbolize the rush to save him.

St Swithun's Day (15 July)
Legend says that if it rains on this day it will continue to do so for 40 days and 40 nights.

Raksha Bandhan (July/August)
A Hindu festival when girls tie a rakhi (bracelet) around their brothers' wrists to protect them, and the brothers promise to protect their sisters.

Ganesh-chaturthi (August/September)
This Hindu festival celebrates the birth of the elephant-headed god Ganesh. Huge statues of the god are made.

Yom Kippur (September)
Jewish festival spent fasting and asking God for forgiveness. A 'shofar' (horn) is blown at the end of the festival.

Chinese Moon Festival (September)

This Chinese festival remembers Chang Er, the wife of a wicked emperor who flew to the moon when her husband tried to kill her. Moon cakes are eaten on this day.

Sukkot (also known as 'The Feast of Tabernacles') (September/October)

This is a Jewish festival when Sukkahs – temporary shelters decorated with fruit and vegetables – are erected in gardens in memory of the exodus from Egypt. Most meals are eaten in the sukkah.

Harvest Festival (September/October)

A time of thanksgiving for the harvesting of crops. Traditions include harvest suppers and giving of food to the needy.

Navaratri (September/October)

Hindu festival celebrating the victory of Rama over the demon king Ravana after nine days and nights of fighting.

Divali (October/November)

Hindus remember the story of Rama and Sita. Sikhs celebrate the sixth Guru, Guru Hargobind's escape from imprisonment. Homes are decorated with divas (lamps).

Bonfire Night (5 November)

A British celebration, sometimes called 'Guy Fawkes Night', which remembers a historical event when a group of men led by Guy Fawkes attempted to blow up the Houses of Parliament in 1605.

Hanukkah (November/December)

A Jewish festival of light lasting eight days, commemorating the reclamation of the temple from the Syrians and the miracle of the temple light that burned for eight days on a small amount of oil. For eight evenings, one candle is lit, from right to left in a hanukiah (nine-branched menorah). Children play a game of dreidel.

Advent (December)

Christian period of preparation for Jesus' birth, beginning on the fourth Sunday before Christmas and ending on Christmas Day. Traditions include Advent candles and calendars.

Christmas Day (25 December)

Christian festival celebrating the birth of Jesus. People decorate their homes and exchange gifts as a reminder of those given to Jesus.

Eid-ul-Fitr (December/January)

Muslim festival held at the end of Ramadan. People wear new clothes, visit family and friends and exchange gifts and cards.

New Year (1 January)

New Year is celebrated with parties and the traditional singing of 'Auld Lang Syne'. People reflect on the past and make resolutions for the future.

Ganjitsu (1 January)

Japanese New Year festival when cards are exchanged on New Year's Day and the first visit of the year is paid to local Shinto shrines.

Saraswati Puja (January)

Widely celebrated in North India, this Hindu festival celebrates Saraswati, goddess of learning and the arts, and marks the beginning of spring. Many children start school on this day.

Chinese New Year (January/February)

The most important Chinese festival, lasting 15 days. People clean and decorate their homes, wear new clothes, visit their friends and family and exchange gifts.

Mardi Gras/Shrove Tuesday (February/March).

Falls on the day before the Christian period of Lent. People use up certain foods to make pancakes, and celebrations include carnivals.

Rain splashes on me

What you need
Pale grey, blue or white A4 paper to make two or three large raindrops per child; blue, black and grey writing materials; white A3 card; sticky tape; cotton; hole-punch; large sheet of paper; easel or flip chart; table.

Preparation
Cut each sheet of A4 paper into a large raindrop shape. Make a hole near the top and bottom of each raindrop using the hole-punch. Cut a cloud shape from the white A3 card.

What to do
Encourage the children to tell you about rain. Ask, 'What does it do?', 'What does it look like?' and 'How does it make you feel?'. Write the key words onto the large sheet of paper.

Explain to the children that they are going to make some rain poems. Show them the cloud and the raindrops. Spread two or three of them out on the table in a line underneath each other. Tell the children that you would like them to write their poems in the raindrops, which will then be joined up with pieces of cotton and hung underneath the cloud to look like rain.

Help the children to decide verbally what they want their descriptive rain poems to be about. Encourage them to use the rain words and phrases that you wrote on the large piece of paper. Ask the children to write their poems on at least two or three raindrops (each raindrop does not have to be filled with writing). Encourage the children to think about the spelling and shape of each word that they write.

When the poems are finished, check the order that the raindrops should be read in and join them together through the holes with lengths of cotton. Tape the cotton at the top of the first raindrop to the back of the cloud shape. Attach the cloud and raindrops to a display board or hang them from the ceiling as a mobile.

Support
Ask the children to draw a 'rainy day' picture on just one raindrop and to describe it to you. Scribe each child's ideas underneath their picture.

Extension
Encourage the children to write longer poems, perhaps including rhymes and using dictionaries to check their spellings.

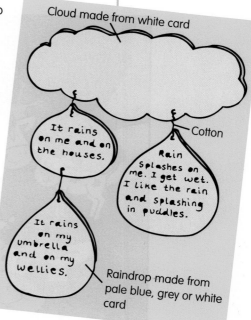

Cloud made from white card

It rains on me and on the houses.

Rain splashes on me. I get wet. I like the rain and splashing in puddles.

It rains on my umbrella and on my wellies.

Cotton

Raindrop made from pale blue, grey or white card

Babies everywhere

What you need
A copy of the photocopiable sheet on page 65; a selection of farm picture books.

Preparation
Familiarize yourself with the story on the photocopiable sheet before carrying out the activity.

What to do
Invite all the children to sit down comfortably in front of you, and sit down yourself so that everyone can see you. Begin by asking if anyone has ever visited a farm. If the children have, ask them about the types of animals that they saw. If the children have not been to a farm, you may want to show them some of the farm books and talk about the different animals that live on a farm.

Tell the children that you are going to read a story called 'Babies everywhere' and that it is about some children, just like them, who go to visit a farm. Explain that you would like them to listen carefully to the story as you tell it.

Read the story to the group using different voices for each character. The story reading can be used as an opportunity to ask the children to predict 'what happens next', or to compare the story with their own experiences.

When you have finished reading the story, talk with the children about what they heard. Ask questions such as, 'Where did all the animals live?', 'Do they all eat the same type of food?' and 'How many chicks and pigs were there in the story?'. The photocopiable page could also be used as a stimulus for some simple drama work, for example, walking across a muddy farmyard or milking a cow.

Support
Read through the story once without stopping. Then re-read it, this time stopping to ask questions about it and encouraging the children to engage in discussions and to predict what they think will happen.

Extension
As you read the story, omit the descriptive parts and encourage individual children to tell the rest of the group what they think each animal would look like.

Dusters, polishes and brushes

What you need
Red, brown, pink or grey A1 sugar paper; white A4 paper; drawing or writing materials; sticky tape; glue; scissors.

Preparation
Draw a large outline of a house showing the walls, roof and chimney onto the sugar paper, and then mark on a horizontal line across the width of the house to separate the first floor and the ground floor. Draw five rooms (bedroom, bathroom, lounge, dining room and kitchen) onto the sugar paper and cut a piece of white paper to fit inside each room.

What to do
Explain that spring is a time for new beginnings when baby animals are born and plants grow new leaves and flowers. Tell the children that people sometimes give their houses a thorough tidy and clean in springtime, which is called a 'spring clean'.

Talk with the children about the types of activities that their parents and carers do to clean the house. Are there any household jobs that the children are allowed to help with?

Give each child the name of a different room in the house, such as kitchen or bedroom, and ask them to think of something that could be done to help clean that room. For example, in the bathroom, the toilet could be cleaned, or the bed could be made in the bedroom.

Ask each child to write their room name and the cleaning job on a piece of white paper that you have cut to fit inside the rooms of the house. The children could also add appropriate illustrations. Glue the pieces of paper onto the corresponding rooms.

Once the children have finished their writing, talk about the things that they would need to do the cleaning, such as dusters, brushes and polishes. On a separate piece of white paper, write 'We need…'. Pass the piece of paper to each child so that they can write, underneath the heading, the names of the cleaning materials that they would need. Tape the shopping list to the bottom of the house.

Support
Label each piece of white paper with the appropriate room name before starting the activity. Let the children write at their own level, using a scribe if necessary.

Extension
Encourage the children to write more about their rooms and to use dictionaries to check spellings.

Learning objective
To make a list as a reminder of tasks to do and objects needed.

Group size
Small group.

Home links
Ask parents and carers to include their children as much as they can in a safe way with household jobs, such as polishing, and to talk to them about what they are doing.

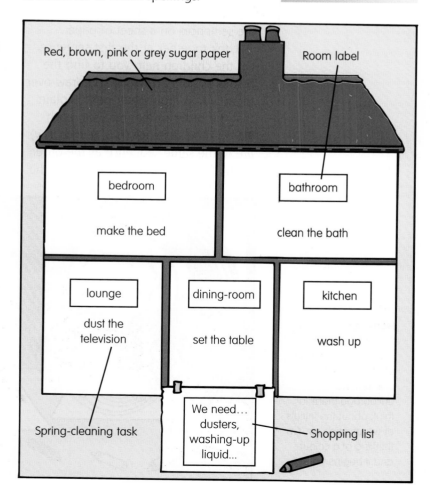

Red, brown, pink or grey sugar paper — Room label

bedroom — make the bed

bathroom — clean the bath

lounge — dust the television

dining-room — set the table

kitchen — wash up

We need… dusters, washing-up liquid…

Spring-cleaning task — Shopping list

Robin Oliver yawned

Learning objective
To hear and say initial sounds in words and recognize some of the letters of the alphabet.

Group size
Small group.

What you need
The photocopiable sheet on page 66; writing materials; highlighter pen; colour picture of a rainbow; paper.

Preparation
Make enough copies of the photocopiable sheet so each child can have one, with two or three spares.

What to do
Look with the children at the picture of the rainbow and talk about its colours and their order. Explain that sometimes people use special sentences (mnemonics) to help them remember things, such as lists of objects.

Read the following sentences to the group: 'Robin Oliver yawned gluing buttons in vests', 'Rashid offered Yasmin gorgeous blooms in vases', 'Running over yaks, growled Boris, is vile'. Write the sentences on a sheet of paper.

Look together at the first sentence. Let the children help you to find the first letters of each word and draw over them with a highlighter pen. Explain that the order of the initials of each word in the sentence (r, o, y, g, b, i, v) are in the same sequence as the order of the first letters of each colour in the rainbow – red, orange, yellow, green, blue, indigo, violet.

As a group, make up a sentence containing seven words whose initials correspond to the ones of the colours of the rainbow in the right order. Write this sentence onto one of the photocopiable sheets, matching each word to its correct initial.

Give each child a copy of the photocopiable sheet and some writing materials. Help the children to write their own rainbow sentences, using the letters on the sheet as a prompt. Encourage the children to say out loud possible words and talk about their initial sounds.

Support
Let the children draw on either side of the letters, using the whole space, two objects that begin with two of the letters (for example, a boat and a yo-yo).

Extension
Give the children a copy of the photocopiable sheet without the letters on it. Encourage them to recite one of the rainbow sentences to help them remember the order of the colours and initial letters.

Home links
Ask parents and carers to play games at home with their children that encourage them to think about the initials of words such as, 'I'm thinking of a colour and it begins with g'.

White rabbits

What you need
A story-book to read to the children such as *I Don't Want to Go to Bed* by Julie Sykes (Little Tiger Press). Choose a book that does not mention rabbits.

Preparation
Read through the story-book and decide on a place where you can stop reading the story and say 'white rabbits' with the minimum of interruption to the story. Initially, say the phrase at a natural pause in the story such as at the end of a sentence.

What to do
Tell the children that, traditionally, it is considered very lucky if the first words that you say to someone on the first of March is 'white rabbits'. Explain that whenever they hear you say 'white rabbits', you would like everyone to turn to the person next to them, shake hands (or give them a hug) and say 'white rabbits'. Let the children practise shaking hands and repeating the phrase 'white rabbits'.

Read the story to the children in the way that you normally would, for example, showing the pictures, encouraging prediction, asking questions and so on. At the point that you decided on, say 'white rabbits'. See how many of the children also say 'white rabbits' and shake hands with each other. You may need to repeat the phrase for anyone who was not listening carefully the first time!

Make this a regular game by choosing a word or phrase from a dictionary and discussing with the group how the word is spelled, its meaning and how the word can be used. Ask the children to do a pre-arranged action whenever you mention the word. Say the word at some point later in the session for the children to respond to.

Support
Tell the children beforehand that you will say 'white rabbits' during the story so that they will be listening out for these words.

Extension
Choose a book about pets or rabbits, such as *Rabbits* by Michaela Miller (*Pets* series, Heinemann), which includes the phrase 'white rabbits' or has pictures of white rabbits that you can talk about with the children.

Learning objective
To listen carefully to language in their environment and to respond to what they hear.

Group size
Large or small group.

Home links
Ask parents and carers to play games and sing songs that will encourage their children to listen and respond, such as 'Simon says...' or 'If you're happy and you know it'.

There's a daffodil

Learning objective
To interact with others
and take turns in
conversation.

Group size
Large or small group.

What you need
A book about spring such as *Spring* by
Nicola Baxter (Franklin Watts); paper or
card; drawing and writing materials.

Preparation
Plan a route around your local area two
or three days in advance and look for
signs of spring, such as new growth,
which you can show to the children.
Arrange extra adult help if necessary.

What to do
Look together at the book about spring
and talk about what happens in spring.
Explain to the children that you are
going to go on a walk around the local
area to look for the signs that spring
has started.

Divide the children into small groups
with a similar number of children in
each group. Give each group an open-
ended challenge of something to find
when out on the walk such as 'find two
different types of yellow flowers' or
'look for hedges sprouting new leaves '.

To help the children remember what
you have asked them to look for, give
each group a picture of the sign of
spring that you want them to find, or a
card with the challenge written on it.

Go for a walk with the children
around your pre-planned route.
Encourage them to look for the signs of
spring around them using all of their
senses. Ask them to show each other
the signs that they find.

On returning to your setting,
ask the children to sit together in
one group. Ask each of the
smaller groups to stand up one
after the other and to tell
everyone else what they were
asked to find, and whether or
not they did. Invite the
'audience' to ask them relevant
questions. If necessary, remind
the children to wait for a break
in the conversation before they
begin speaking.

Support
Sit the children in a circle and
ask each child in turn to talk
about the signs of spring that
they saw and heard during the
walk. Encourage the children
who are not talking to put their
hands up if they want to ask a
question, and to wait until the
other person has finished talking before
they can start speaking.

Extension
Encourage the children to think about
their audience when talking about the
walk and to speak slowly and clearly.

Home links
Ask parents and
carers to encourage
their children to take
part in conversations.

Snake begins with 's'

What you need
Green sugar paper or thin card; writing materials; safety scissors; flat round object to draw around, such as a small plate; stapler; cotton.

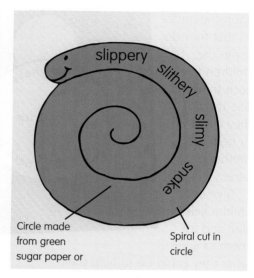

slippery

slithery

slimy

snake

Circle made from green sugar paper or

Spiral cut in circle

Preparation
Draw around the small plate on the green sugar paper or card to make a circle and cut it out. You will need one disc for every child and one extra to make a sample 'snake'. Draw a wide spiral on one of the discs, starting at the left-hand side of the circumference and finishing at the disc's centre. Cut along the lines.

What to do
Tell the children that St Patrick is remembered because he sent all the snakes in Ireland into the Irish Sea. Show the children the spiral that you have made. Hold the edge of the disc in one hand and pull its centre downwards with the other hand to stretch the spiral and make a 'snake'. Help the children to draw their own spirals and cut along the lines. Encourage them to draw an eye onto their snake at the edge of the disc where the spiral begins. Starting at the 'head' (near the eye), ask the children

to write the word 'snake' from left to right, writing towards the snake's tail at the centre of the disc.

Talk with the group about the initial sound of 'snake'. Encourage the children to think of more words beginning with the letter 's'. Words could be snake-related, such as 'slippery', 'slimy' and 'slithery', or everyday words such as 'shape', 'star' and 'shop'. Ask the children to choose some of these words and to write them onto their snakes after the word 'snake', following the spiral left to right towards the snake's tail. Staple a piece of cotton to the top of each snake and hang them from the ceiling. Encourage the children to look at each other's snakes, reading the words from left to right.

Support
Make the children's snakes in advance and let the children write fewer words on them.

Extension
Encourage the children to think of as many two- and three-syllable words beginning with 's' as possible.

Learning objective
To know that print in English is read from left to right.

Group size
Small group.

Home links
Ask parents and carers to think of a letter sound and to challenge the children to name as many words as possible that begin with that sound.

Flower cards

What you need
Brightly coloured card; yellow card; small circular object such as a small plate; pencil; drawing and writing materials; scissors; glue.

Preparation
You will need one yellow disc, flower shape and card strip for each child. Using the small circular object as a template, cut some discs from the yellow card to make centres for flowers. Write 'I can help' around the top of each disc. Draw some simple flower shapes, their centres being larger than the yellow discs, on the brightly coloured card and cut these out. Also, cut some strips of brightly coloured card the length of the flower and the width of one of the petals. Fold each strip in half horizontally along the short edge.

What to do
Remaining sensitive to individual circumstances, explain to the children that, traditionally, Mother's Day is a time when children show their mothers their love and appreciation for all that they do. Invite the children to each think of one thing that they could do to help their mother or carer.

Give each child a yellow disc and ask them to write what they could do to help their mother or carer in its centre. Encourage the children to do as much of the writing as possible by themselves and to say the letters and words out loud as they write them.

Help the children to glue each disc onto a flower shape. Stand the flowers up by gluing half of a folded strip (crease pointing to the top of the flower) onto the back of each flower.

Let the children give the flowers as Mother's Day cards by writing 'Happy Mother's Day' around the bottom of each yellow disc.

Support
Help the children to say aloud the words that they want to write, and scribe for them if necessary. Provide lots of clues about the phonic components of each word.

Extension
Leave the yellow discs blank and ask the children to try writing all the words by themselves. Encourage them to use longer, more complex words.

Red square

What you need

At least 30 blank playing cards; eight to 12 paint charts showing several shades of red; two or three pieces of white A3 card; several objects of different shades of red strategically placed around the room; scissors; glue; marker pen.

Preparation

Cut out as many shades of red and their names as possible from one paint chart. Glue one colour and its name onto each blank playing card to make one set of colour cards. Do this with each paint chart so that every player has one playing card for each colour.

Cut a strip of white card the height of a playing card, but equal in length to the number of different colour cards. Divide the strip with the marker pen into the number of appropriate playing-card-sized spaces. Write one colour name into each space. Make a strip for every player.

What to do

Explain that red is important in Holi celebrations because the colour is thought to bring luck. Encourage the children to each find something that is red and, together, look at the items. Tell the children that although they are all red, each shade of red has a name. Give each child a set of 'red' playing cards and a card strip. Read the colour names together.

Mix up the playing cards and spread them out on the table with the colours face down. Let each child individually turn over two colour cards. If the colours are the same, the child takes both of them and puts them on top of the appropriate name on the card strip. If the cards do not match, the cards are turned face down and the next player has a turn. The winner is the first person to cover all the colours on their card strip.

Use the cards as a 'dictionary' for creative writing, or display them near the art area so that the children can use them when they work. Carry out the game using other colours, too.

Support

Give the children fewer colours to find and choose colours with short names that can easily be read phonetically.

Extension

Encourage the children to read the words independently as they turn the cards over.

Square of colour taken from a paint chart

White card

Name of colour

| burgundy | red | maroon |

| red | wine | burgundy | maroon | scarlet | cherry |

Name of colour

Playing card

cherry   scarlet   wine

In the egg

What you need
Five to ten hollow plastic eggs that can
be separated into halves; several small
toys and objects that will fit into the
closed plastic eggs; strips of paper;
writing materials.

Preparation
Hide an object or toy in two or three
plastic eggs. Write short sentences on
the strips of paper to describe the
hidden objects. You will need between
two and five descriptive sentences for
each toy. For example, descriptions
about a ball could include, 'It is red and
bounces', or 'I like throwing and
catching it'.

What to do
Tell the children that chocolate eggs are
often eaten at Easter as a reminder of
new life and how Jesus Christ rose from
the dead. Show the children the closed
plastic eggs where you have put the
small objects. Explain that you have
hidden some items in the eggs and that
you would like the children to guess
what they are. Invite them to have a
few guesses.

Show the children a clue for one of
the toys and help them to read the
sentence. Continue giving written clues
until the children can decide what is
hidden in each egg.

Give each child an egg, pen or
pencil, some strips of paper and,
without the others seeing, an object to
hide in their egg. Ask each child to
write some clues about the appearance,
shape, size or usage of the object. Let
the children take it in turns to guess
what is inside each egg by reading the
written clues.

Encourage the children to find other
objects to put inside the eggs and to
write descriptive clues. Play the game
in reverse by hiding certain objects
around your setting and placing the
clues about each object's identity and
hiding place inside the eggs.

Support
Ask the children to tell you their clues
for you to scribe. Encourage them to
keep the descriptions short and simple.
Read the clues together as a group.

Extension
Invite the children to write longer clue
sentences. Encourage them to use as
many of their senses as possible to
describe the object.

Next was a plague of frogs

What you need
Large, open floor space; brightly coloured chalk; the photocopiable sheet on page 67; props to recreate home life such as tables, chairs and plates (optional).

Preparation
Draw a line dividing the floor space equally into two. At opposite corners

across the dividing line, draw a square on the floor, large enough for several children to stand in at the same time. If using tables, chairs and plates, put these into the squares to make two 'houses'.

What to do
Read the different plagues on the photocopiable sheet to the children. Explain that all the horrible things in the ten plagues happened to the Egyptians, but not to the Israelites.

Divide the children into two groups. Explain that one group will be the Egyptians and one group will be the Israelites. Talk with the children about each of the plagues and provide help for each group with deciding on the suitable actions that they could perform when each of the plagues are mentioned. For example, for 'plague of blood', the children could pretend to drink and then pull faces at the taste of the water, or for the 'plague of lice', they could pretend to scratch themselves.

Ask the Egyptians to stand on one side of the divide in one 'house' and the Israelites in the other 'house'. Re-read the photocopiable sheet to the children. For each plague, ask the groups to do the actions that you agreed on before the start of the activity. Remind the children that for each of the plagues it was only the Egyptians that suffered; the Jews were unaffected. At the end of the tenth plague, ask the Egyptians and the Israelites to swap roles. Encourage the children to join in as much as possible with the retelling of the story.

Support
Rather than dividing the group into two, ask all the children to do the same actions while you read through the list of plagues.

Extension
Re-create an Egyptian house in the role-play area. Give the children a copy of the plagues and ask them to retell the story.

Learning objective
To retell the narrative in the correct sequence.

Group size
Large group.

Home links
Explain to the children what the Pesach meal is. Ask parents and carers to talk with their children about any special meals that their family may have, such as Christmas or Divali.

The gilip squibbled

Learning objective
To explore and experiment with sounds, words and texts.

Group size
Small group.

What you need
The photocopiable sheet on page 68; pastel-coloured A4 paper; writing materials; brightly coloured A3 sugar paper; glue; spreaders.

Preparation
Copy the photocopiable sheet and read it two or three times to familiarize yourself with the rhymes.

What to do
Explain to the children that April Fool's Day is traditionally a time for playing tricks on other people and telling jokes and nonsense rhymes, but only until midday. Read the rhymes on the photocopiable sheet to the children. Talk with them about the rhymes. Do they make sense? Discuss the words that the children know. Do they know all of them? What do the children think the words mean?

Tell the children that you would like them to make up some silly nonsense rhymes of their own. The rhymes could either combine strange objects in unusual places, such as 'there was a pink cat that lived in a cup and liked to tickle a purple pup', or the rhymes could be made up completely of nonsense words, such as 'the gilip squibbled as the piboor rimbled'.

Give each child a pastel-coloured sheet of A4 paper and ask them to write independently, but to talk with each other about their ideas and what they are writing.

Encourage the children to 'sound out' the words as they write them.

When the rhymes are finished, ask each child to choose a piece of brightly coloured sugar paper to stick their poem onto. Help them to draw a large shape (larger than the paper that the rhyme is written on) and to cut it out. The shape could be an object mentioned in the rhyme, a fantastical animal, or just a strange shape. Glue the rhyme onto the sugar paper.

Support
Make up one nonsense rhyme as a group. Ask the children to experiment with the sounds of the words by changing the initial sounds of each word or to adapt an existing rhyme.

Extension
Encourage the children to write longer poems, possibly including more rhymes, and to try to make up more nonsense words.

Kangaroos and koalas

What you need
Large wooden or card letter templates; white A4 paper; brightly coloured A3 sugar paper; glue; marker pen.

Preparation
Make a list of the initial letters of the first name of everyone in the group.

that all begin with the letter 'K' – the Kachera (shorts), Kirpan (short sword), Kesh (uncut hair), Kangha (comb) and the Kara (steel bracelet).

Give each child the sugar paper letter that matches the initial of their first name and five of the small pieces of white paper. Ask the children to try to think of five things that are special to them and which begin with the same sound as the first letter in their name. For example, Katrina might like her toy kangaroo, her keyboard, her kite, her kitten and her play kitchen. Ask the children to draw and label one of their special objects on each piece of paper. Help the children to glue the finished pictures onto their sugar-paper letters. Compile all the letters into a book and encourage the children to look at the book together and to read the letters and the labels for each picture.

Using the list as a guide, find the letter templates that match each initial. Draw around each letter template onto the brightly coloured sugar paper and cut them out. Fold each sheet of A4 paper in half and then in half again. Open out the paper and cut along the folds to make four smaller pieces of paper.

What to do
Explain to the children that Baisakhi is an important time for new Sikhs as this is when they first receive the five Ks. These are very special to Sikhs and are taken everywhere. The five Ks take their name from the initials of five objects

Support
Encourage the children to draw five of their favourite objects, not necessarily beginning with the same letter as their first name, and scribe the labels for their objects.

Extension
Ask the children to write a detailed sentence about their favourite object.

Learning objective
To use a pencil and
hold it effectively to
form recognizable
letters, most of which
are correctly formed.

Group size
Small group.

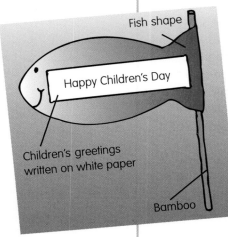

Fish shape

Happy Children's Day

Children's greetings
written on white paper

Bamboo

Home links
Ask parents and
carers to help their
children to make
banners or greetings
cards for special
events at home such
as birthdays or
parties.

Flying fish

What you need
Scissors; thick card; brightly coloured tissue paper; plain white paper; glue; bamboo canes; bucket; writing materials; sticky tape; gummed-paper shapes.

Preparation
Draw a simple fish shape onto the thick card. Cut this out and use it as a template to draw fish shapes onto the tissue paper. You will need one fish for each child. Cut out the tissue-paper fishes.

What to do
Explain that Kodomono-hi (Japanese Children's Day) was originally known as Boy's Day. Parents used to make banners in the shape of fish with good-luck messages written on them for their sons.

Tell the children that you would like each of them to make their own fish banner for Children's Day. Show the group one of the fish that you have cut from the tissue paper. Talk about the types of things that could be written on the banner. These could be messages wishing one another 'Happy Children's Day', 'Good luck' or simply 'Thank you Richard for being my friend'.

Encourage each child to tell you what message they want to write on their fish. Suggest that the children try to keep their messages short. Give everyone a piece of plain white paper to write their message on. Check each child's pencil grip regularly and correct if necessary. Encourage the children to think

about how to form each letter as they write it.

Help the children to glue their messages onto their tissue-paper fish and to add gummed shapes for the fish eyes and mouth. To display the fish, glue or tape each of the fish tails onto separate bamboo poles (if necessary, curl the edge of the tail around the pole slightly). Stand the poles carefully in a bucket so that they will not fall over, but so that the fish heads can move gently in the breeze.

Support
Encourage the children to write independently at their own level or scribe each child's message onto a separate sheet of paper for them to look at as they write.

Extension
Ask the children to think about the size of their letters and the lengths of the ascenders and descenders (stalks or stems and tails!).

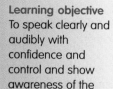

Come and visit

What you need
Some brochures about local attractions and things to do in your area from the tourist information centre or alternatively borrow some pictorial local interest books from the library; flip chart; marker pen.

What to do
Talk with the children about what they do during their summer holidays. Do any of the children go away on holiday? Be sensitive to individual circumstances. Explain that before people go on holiday they sometimes like to find out about the place they want to visit and what they can do there. Look together at the tourist information brochures and find out where your local places of interest are.

Talk together about other things that people can do, see or visit in your area, such as go to the park, catch a bus into town or visit a farm. Write some of the children's ideas on the flip chart so that they can refer back to them later. Explain to the children that you would like them, one at time, to tell the others what they like to do in the local area,

why it is so special and why it should be visited.

As the children take turns to talk, encourage them to speak slowly and clearly so that everyone else in the group can understand what they are saying. If appropriate, record the talks onto a tape recorder or video camera.

Develop the activity further by asking the children to each choose somewhere locally that interests them. Provide help to each child with finding out all they can about that location using the tourist information brochures and local interest books. Encourage them to talk about the place that they have chosen, giving as much information about it as possible.

Support
Begin by asking each child to say just one thing that is good about their local area. If the children need more confidence, they could work in pairs.

Extension
Encourage the children to make 'notes' about what they are going to say, and to check them throughout their talk.

Learning objective
To speak clearly and audibly with confidence and control and show awareness of the listener.

Group size
Small group.

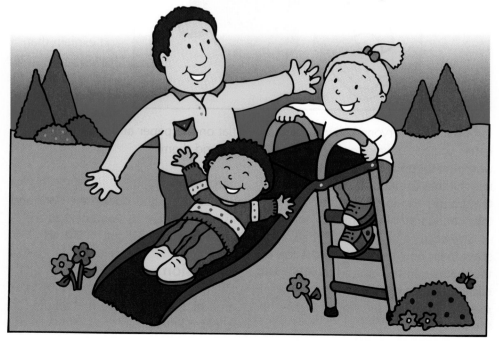

Home links
Ask parents and carers to encourage their children to talk audibly and clearly about what they can see around them when they are out and about.

Shadow letters

What you need
Concrete or tarmac area; a selection of large thick wooden or foam lower-case letters that can stand up on end by themselves; brightly coloured chalk.

What to do
On a bright, sunny day, take the children outside onto a concrete or tarmac area that is not in any shade. Give each child two or three letters.

Check that everyone knows which letters you have given to them and where the bottom of each letter is. Ask the children to stand their letters up on the ground and invite them to look at the shadows that these make.

Give each child a piece of chalk and show them how to trace over the top of the shadow on the ground to write each letter. Then, ask the children to make a circle with the wooden letters in the middle of it.

Invite the children to walk around the circle in a particular direction. Explain that when you call out a letter, everyone must run into the circle and try to find the letter that you called out. The child who finds it takes it to a space and writes the letter on top of its shadow. Once the player has written the letter, he or she can put it back in the middle of the circle and join in the game again. (More than one child at once could write letters to speed up the game.)

When there are two or three of each of the letters written on the ground, call out a letter and ask the whole group to find and stand on the appropriate chalk letter rather than drawing it.

Next, invite the children to play the game indoors. In a spacious area, tape a large sheet of paper to the floor and explain that, instead of using the shadow to write the letter, the children must lay the letters flat on the paper and draw directly around them.

Support
Spread the letters out on the floor and ask the children to stand next to the letter that you call out.

Extension
Call out 'blends' such as 'sh' and 'cl' and ask the children to find all the relevant letters.

Learning objective
To link sounds to letters.

Group size
Small group.

Home links
Ask parents and carers to help their children to look for letters around the home (on clothing labels, for example) and to 'read' them by saying aloud their sounds.

Sun and flower

What you need
Marker pen; 30 to 40 blank playing cards; white A4 paper.

Preparation
On the sheet of A4 paper, make a list of as many compound words as possible that can be split in half to make two smaller words, such as 'sunflower' (sun and flower), 'snowball' (snow and ball), 'teaspoon' (tea and spoon) or 'football' (foot and ball). Referring to the list that you have made, write each of the smaller words onto the individual playing cards.

What to do
Explain to the children that some long words are actually two short words put together. Show the children two or three of the compound words on your list. Read them together and challenge the children to say what they think the smaller words are in each of your longer words.

Look at the words on the playing cards and check that each child can read every word. Spread the playing cards out on the floor or a table. Give the children a time limit, such as five minutes, and ask them to make as many long words as possible by putting together two playing cards. At the end of the time, let the children take it in turns to read out the longer words that they have made. Some of them might be completely nonsensical!

Invite the children to look again at the words that they made. Challenge them to make up more long words, using only the cards that they collected, by swapping around the last cards of each long word – for example, 'sunflower' could now become 'sunball' or 'sunspoon'.

Extend the activity by spreading out the cards and asking the children to pair the correct words together.

Support
Write on the playing cards only words that the children can read and provide fewer playing cards.

Extension
Once the children have carried out the activity, give them some blank playing cards to write on a selection of short words which can then be combined to make compound words.

Learning objective
To explore and experiment with words, especially word endings.

Group size
Small group.

Home links
Give each child ten playing cards with words written on (five pairs of words). Explain the game to parents and carers and ask them to help the children to make up five long words using the ten cards.

Minibeast rhymes

What you need
Writing and drawing materials; white A4 paper; a selection of books about minibeasts, such as *Minibeasts* by Brian Moses (Macmillan Children's Books); the photocopiable sheet on page 69; green sugar paper.

Preparation
Copy the photocopiable sheet and read through the rhymes several times.

What to do
Read the rhymes on the photocopiable sheet to the children. Did they notice anything special about them? Re-read the rhymes. Give each child a copy of the photocopiable sheet and look together at the words at the end of each line. Say aloud pairs of rhyming words and talk about how the words sound the same, but have a different initial sound.

Give each child a sheet of A4 paper and a pencil and explain that you would like them to make up a rhyme about a minibeast. The children could look through the minibeast books that you collected for ideas. Ask each child to think of two sentences about their minibeast with rhyming words at the end. Suggest that the children use short, simple rhymes such as 'sun' and 'fun', or 'log' and 'dog'. Encourage them to sound out the words, and especially the rhymes, as they write them.

When the children have finished writing their rhymes, help them to trim around the edge of their poem (leaving a slight margin). Mount the rhymes onto minibeast-shaped pieces of paper and display on a large tree shape made from green and brown sugar paper.

Alternatively, help the children to use the minibeast books to discover where the creatures could be found – for example, woodlice like dark places, ants stay on the ground and butterflies like to fly. Put the poems around your setting in places where the minibeasts might be found, such as on windows or hiding under a chair, but make sure that the rhymes can still be read!

Support
Help the children to compose a group minibeast rhyme which you can scribe for them.

Extension
Encourage the children to make up more sentences for their rhymes.

At the beach

What you need

Role-play area or large open space; sticky tape; large sheet or roll of yellow paper; large sheet or roll of pale blue paper; two or three deckchairs or a blanket; buckets; spades; sea shells; picnic hamper with plates and 'pretend' food; sun-glasses; empty bottle of sun block; sun-hats; books about the

seaside such as *At the Seaside* by Karen Bryant-Mole (*Images* series, Heinemann).

Preparation

In the role-play area, tape the yellow paper to the floor to make a 'beach' and tape the blue paper next to the beach to make the 'sea'. Put the seaside items on the beach.

What to do

Ask the children if any of them have ever been to the seaside. Be sensitive to individual circumstances. Encourage the children to talk about their experiences and what they saw and did at the

seaside. If none of the children have been to a beach, look together at the seaside books that you collected and talk about what people do when they visit the coast.

Take the children to the role-play area and explain that the yellow section is the beach and the blue section represents the sea. Initially, work with the children to re-enact some of the events that might happen on a beach, such as a sand-castle-building competition or sharing a picnic with the family. Encourage the children to pretend to be someone at the beach (a parent, a child, a life-guard) and to play together as a group.

Extend the role-play by adding objects that the children might see at the beach, such as a 'puppet theatre' to re-create 'Punch and Judy' shows, or an ice-cream van made from a large painted cardboard box. Make a display of books showing the things that people do at the seaside or the animals that can be found there.

Support

Work with smaller groups of children and introduce lots of vocabulary that the children will need to role-play being at the seaside.

Extension

Ask the children to suggest things that could be added to the seaside to improve the role-play.

Tomato book

What you need
Flip chart; sheet of red sugar paper; gold and yellow crayons or pens that can be seen on the red paper; knife; chopping board; three or four tomatoes; small plate; scissors; length of green ribbon.

Preparation
Using a pencil, draw around the small plate on the sheet of red sugar paper

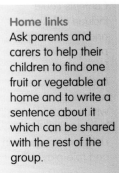

several times and cut out the discs (one for each child).

What to do
Show the children a tomato. Encourage them to tell you something about the tomato, such as its colour, size and shape. Write the children's comments on the flip chart.

Carefully, cut the tomato in half. Look together at the inside of the tomato and ask the children to describe what they can see. Write the children's

observations on the flip chart. Give each child a piece of the tomato to hold (and eat if desired). Ask them to describe what it feels or tastes like, and add their remarks to the flip chart.

Give each child a red sugar-paper disc and a gold or yellow crayon or pen. Ask them to write something about the way that the tomato looks, feels, smells or tastes in a sentence such as 'The tomato is red and round and soft', rather than just saying, 'red and round and soft'.

Once the children have finished writing, gather up the red pieces of paper. Punch a hole near the top of each disc at approximately the same place on every disc. Put the discs together, thread a length of green ribbon through the holes and knot the ends together on the outside to make a book. Trim the ends to look like a tomato stalk. Make a 'tomato' display with the books, some cut tomatoes and pictures of the fruit or empty seed packets.

Try making shaped books for other seasonal fruit and vegetables such as pumpkins in autumn or Brussels sprouts in winter.

Support
Scribe the sentences for the children if necessary. Encourage them to tell you their ideas in a sentence.

Extension
Introduce the children to sentence conventions such as capital letters and full stops and encourage them to use them in their sentence.

Buddha's life

What you need
A sheet of white A3 paper for each child; drawing and writing materials; a book about the life of Buddha such as *I am a Buddhist* by Dhanapala Samarasekara (*My Belief* series, Franklin Watts).

Preparation
Fold each of the A3 sheets of paper vertically into three (top, middle and bottom). Read through the book several times to familiarize yourself with the story of Buddha's life.

What to do
Explain to the children that the festival of Wesak celebrates the life and beliefs of Buddha who founded the Buddhist religion. Tell them that you are going to read them a story about Buddha and that you would like them to listen carefully to it. Encourage the children to ask the meaning of any words that they are unsure about.

Read the book to the children, stopping to explain any unknown words if necessary. Talk with them about what happened in the story and the sequence of events that occurred in Buddha's life.

Give each child a folded sheet of A3 paper and some of the drawing and writing materials. Tell the children that there are three sections on their pieces of paper and that you would like them to write about the three main things that happened to Buddha – his birth, his enlightenment and his death.

Explain to the children that they should write about each event on a different section of the paper: Buddha's birth on the top section, his enlightenment in the middle and his death on the bottom section.

Invite the children to illustrate their work with suitable pictures. Encourage them to draw on their own experiences as inspiration for the pictures of birth and death. For the enlightenment of Buddha, they could show Buddha following some of the Buddhist beliefs such as not hurting animals and being kind to others.

Support
Ask the children to retell the story of Buddha by drawing pictures instead. The children may find it easier to draw or paint three pictures on three separate pieces of paper.

Extension
Encourage the children to write more about Buddha and to use simple dictionaries to check spellings.

Learning objective
To retell a narrative in the correct sequence.

Group size
Small group.

Home links
Ask parents and carers to read a short book such as *This is the Bear* by Sarah Hayes (Walker Books) to the children and then to help them retell the story in their own words.

Milk, yoghurt and cheese

What you need
A selection of empty, clean food cartons, containers and packaging with the labels on them; sheets of paper; safety magnifying glasses.

Preparation
A few days before you carry out this activity, ask parents and carers to give their children two or three empty, clean food cartons or packaging with

ingredients listed on them, such as ice-cream cartons, yoghurt pots or rice pudding labels to bring to the setting.

What to do
Explain to the children that Shavuot is a Jewish festival and that milk-based foods such as blintzes and cheesecake are an important part of the celebrations.

Choose one of the packaging items to show to the children and explain that most food packaging has a list of ingredients saying what was used to make that food. Point out the ingredients on your chosen packaging to the children and explain that the ingredient that was used the most is listed first on the packaging, and the ingredient used the least is at the end of the list.

Look at the ingredients with the children, using the magnifying glasses if necessary. Is milk on the list? Give each child two or three different pieces of packaging to look at. Ask them to read down the list of ingredients, from left to right and from top to bottom, to try to find the word 'milk'.

Talk about which of the foods contains milk. Some of the children may be surprised at just how many different types of food contain milk. Use the packaging to make cow- or milk-bottle-shaped collages.

Support
Choose four or five food packaging items that list milk as an ingredient. Make an enlarged copy of the ingredients of the products for each child and read through each ingredient list together.

Extension
Help the children to use information books to find out about the different types of milk, such as full fat, semi-skimmed, skimmed, goat's and coconut, or milk products such as yoghurt and cheese. Encourage the children to look at the packaging to see how many foods contain each of the different types of milk or milk-based products.

Summer sun shines on and on

What you need
Large, open floor space; the photocopiable sheet on page 70; a book with a picture of Stonehenge such as *Great Britain* (*Dorling Kindersley Travel Guides*, Dorling Kindersley).

Preparation
Make a copy of the photocopiable sheet and learn the words to the song 'Summer sun shines on and on' with the children.

What to do
Explain to the children that on Midsummer's Eve people sometimes meet at Stonehenge and other stone circles. Show the children the picture of Stonehenge. Continue by saying that Midsummer celebrations often include singing and dancing.

Take the children to the large, open floor space and invite them to stand in a circle with their arms outstretched so that only their fingertips touch. Choose a child to be the leader to start the game.

Ask the children to sing the chorus of the song together. The child chosen to start the game must then walk around the outside of the circle, weaving in and out of the other children. At some point, the 'leader' should tap someone on the shoulder. The chosen child then holds hands with the leader and together they must decide on a way to move around the circle such as running, jumping, walking and so on. They then continue around the circle in the manner that they chose while singing the verse. At the end of the verse, the

'leader' stands back in the circle and the chorus is sung again by everyone. The child who was tapped on the shoulder continues to walk around the circle to find a partner. Together they decide on how to move around the circle while singing the verse and so on. Continue until everyone has had a turn, or for as long as desired.

Support
Ask the children to sing the verse only, omitting each chorus. Let all the children join in the singing rather than

just the two children who are moving around the circle.

Extension
Invite the children to think of as many different ways of moving as possible and to try to use and explore all the space available. Also, encourage them to choose children other than just their best friend.

Learning objective
To interact with others and take turns.

Group size
Small or large group.

Home links
Encourage parents and carers to sing action songs with their children such as 'Ring-a-ring-o'-roses'.

About Dad...

What you need
Sheets of white A4 paper; drawing and writing materials; paintbrushes; powder paints; paint palettes; a sheet of A3 sugar paper for each child; a word processor and printer (if available).

Preparation
Fold the sheets of A4 paper horizontally into three. At the top left-hand side of each section, write 'About Dad... '. (If preferred, a word processor could be used to write this.) Cut the paper into three along the folds. Each child will need one of the 'About Dad...' sections.

What to do
Give each child a sheet of A3 sugar paper together with some of the painting materials and ask them to paint a picture of their father large enough to fill the paper. Be sensitive to individual circumstances. If appropriate, the word 'Dad' can be substituted with the name of another special person such as a male carer, an uncle or a brother. Leave the paintings to dry.

Challenge the children to think of as many things as possible that a dad (or their chosen person) does such as 'cooks well', 'tells funny jokes' or 'plays computer games with me'. You may want to write the children's ideas on a piece of paper as they suggest them. Give each child a piece of paper with 'About Dad...' written on it. Ask them to write their ideas underneath the title at their own level of writing. Encourage them to write simple words by themselves, sounding out the parts of the words as they write them.

Help the children to trim the paper with their writing on and to glue this onto their painting. Display the pictures either in a simple book or alongside a display of objects and books that dads might enjoy, such as a football or a book about golf.

Support
Encourage each child to think of one thing that they could say about their father or special person and write this on the 'About Dad...' piece of paper. As you write, talk with the children about the sounds of the words and the individual letters.

Extension
Ask the children to write longer sentences using more complex words. Encourage them to use simple dictionaries to check spellings.

Tell me about the boats

Learning objective
To understand how information can be found in non-fiction texts.

Group size
Small group.

What you need

Non-fiction books about the Chinese Dragon Boat Festival such as *Faiths and Festivals* by Martin Palmer (Ward Lock Educational); two sheets of brightly coloured A4 card; hole-punch; coloured ribbon; sheets of white A4 paper; drawing and writing materials; a word processor and printer (if available).

Preparation

Select some non-fiction books about the Dragon Boat Festival ensuring that some have contents, index and glossary pages. Choose a variety of lengths and difficulties of books. Keep aside one very easy book.

What to do

Ask the children if they have heard of the Chinese Dragon Boat Festival. What do the children think a dragon boat might be? Do they know what happens at the festival?

Explain to the children that you are going to read them a book and that you would like them to listen carefully and to think of some things that they would like to know more about. Read the easy book to the children and when you have finished, encourage them to ask questions such as, 'What are the boats made from?', 'Why do the boats have eyes painted on them?' and so on. Write the children's questions on a piece of paper.

Show the children how to use the index and contents pages in the other information books to answer their questions. Help them to use the books to discover the answers that they want.

Ask each child to write a sentence at their own level about the Dragon Boat Festival or to type a sentence on a word processor. Collect all the children's work and make a book about the festival, adding a contents and index page with the help of the children. Create a cover using the brightly coloured card. Make holes in the left-hand side of every page using the hole-punch and tie the pages and the cover together with the ribbon.

Support

Use the contents page only and provide more help with the writing or using the computer.

Extension

Encourage the children to work more independently with their writing and provide less help with using the contents and index pages.

Home links
Ask parents and carers to encourage their children to think of one question and to help them find the answer in an appropriate non-fiction book using the contents, index and glossary pages.

It's raining

What you need
A dice; a different-coloured counter for each player; the photocopiable sheets on pages 71 and 72; thin card.

Preparation
Copy both of the photocopiable sheets onto the card. If desired, the sheets could be laminated or covered with plastic covering film.

What to do
Explain that St Swithun was a bishop who lived many years ago (in the 9th century) and that he is remembered each year on 15 July. There is a tradition that if it rains on St Swithun's day, it will rain every day for the next forty days!

Show the children the copies of the photocopiable sheets. Let each child choose a coloured counter and then invite the children in turn to roll the dice once. This determines which of the photocopiable sheets are used. If any of the children roll a '4', the wet weather

sheet is played on. If nobody rolls a '4', use the sunny weather sheet. Each sheet consists of 40 days.

Ask all the players to put their counters around the edge on the appropriate sheet. The first square is dated 16 July. The children then take it in turns to roll the dice and move their counter the appropriate number of spaces along the track following the arrows. Once the end of a row is reached, the counter should be moved into the square directly underneath the square that the counter is currently in. If the children land on a square with instructions written on it, then they must read and follow them. Encourage the children to read the words from left to right and top to bottom. If a player rolls a six, they can have another turn, however, only two successive turns are allowed! The first winner is the child to reach the 40th square (24 August).

Support
Help the children to move around the track and to read and follow the instructions.

Extension
Encourage the children to read the instructions on the sheets by themselves and to look carefully at the directions of the arrows.

I can help you

What you need
A very long piece of string or ribbon (approximately five to ten metres, depending on the size of the group).

Preparation
Tie the ends of the string or ribbon together to make a large loop.

What to do
Sit with the children on the floor in a large circle with everyone facing into the centre. Explain that during the festival of Raksha Bandhan, sisters tie a 'rakhi', which is a type of colourful bracelet, around their brother's wrists. In return, the brother offers his protection and help to his sister.

Tell the children that you are going to play a game and you would like everyone to think of something that they could do to help the person that they are sitting next to in the circle. This could be helping to tie someone's shoelaces or reading a book with someone. Encourage the children to tell you their ideas.

Hold the ribbon loop and ask the child sitting next to you to take hold of it. While they do this, tell the child how you can help them. For example, 'I can help Jordan to write his name'. The child who has just taken the ribbon continues to hold it and offers it to the person sitting next to them in the circle while also suggesting something helpful that they could do for them.

Continue around the circle with each child explaining to their neighbour how they could help them and giving them a length of the ribbon to hold. Those who have been given the ribbon must keep hold of it until the end of the game. The game finishes when everyone in the circle is holding the ribbon.

Support
Invite all the children to take hold of the ribbon before the game begins. To make it easier for the children to think of a helpful idea, suggest they choose a way to help a friend or a carer, not necessarily the person that they are sitting next to.

Extension
Encourage the children to say their name and the person who they want to help, for example, 'I am Mary O'Donnell, and I will help Milo to put his bricks away'.

Learning objective
To use talk to clarify thinking, ideas and feelings.

Group size
Large or small group.

Home links
Ask parents and carers to encourage their children to talk about their feeling and thoughts.

Learning objective
To use talk to
organize, sequence
and clarify thinking.

Group size
Small group.

Make a model

What you need
Books with pictures of Ganesh or the statues made for Ganesh-chaturthi such as *I am a Hindu* by Manju Aggarwal (*My belief* series, Franklin Watts); glue; sticky tape; scissors; variety of paints and paintbrushes; large cardboard boxes such as cereal boxes, shoeboxes and so on; scraps of fabric and wool; newspaper; aprons; drawing and writing materials; flip chart.

What to do
Explain to the children that during the Hindu festival of Ganesh-chaturthi, people make tall statues of Ganesh. Show the children the book with the pictures of Ganesh. Encourage them to talk about his appearance.

Tell the children that you would like them to work together to make their own statue of Ganesh. Give each child a piece of A4 paper and some drawing and writing materials which they can use to make 'notes' on at their own level of writing so that they can 'read' them. Ask the children to decide what they think their statue should look like and the things that they could use to make it. Do they think a cereal box would make a good arm or a shoebox an ideal leg or foot? At this point, the children will need to think about just how big they want to make their Ganesh statue, and how they want to join all the body parts together. Scribe the children's thoughts on the flip chart.

Once the children have finished talking about and organizing their model, help them to make it. Everyone in the group should be able to contribute something to the discussions and model-making. Encourage the children to continue talking about Ganesh and what they are doing or how the model could be improved.

Support
Ask the children lots of open-ended questions to encourage them to talk.

Extension
Encourage the children to question what they are doing and to verbally decide on the order in which things should be done.

Home links
Encourage parents and carers to talk with their children about what they are doing when they make models at home, for example, which bricks they are using, where they could put them and so on. Alternatively, ask parents and carers to make simple recipes with their children, such as peppermint creams, that follow instructions and work in a logical sequence.

There's Orion

What you need
Information books about constellations such as *Stars and Planets* by Angela Royston (*First Look Through* series, Heinemann); white A5 paper; marker pen; sheets of black A4 sugar paper; pin; sheet of polystyrene; strips of paper with the alphabet written on in both lower- and upper-case letters.

Preparation
Look through the books to find out the names of some constellations such as

'Orion', 'Cassiopeia' or 'The Great Bear'. Write each name on a separate piece of white paper.

What to do
Explain to the children that as days grow shorter and nights grow longer, we can see the stars and moon earlier in the day than during the summer. Tell the children that stars are sometimes grouped together in constellations such as 'The Great Bear'.

Talk with the children about how contents and index pages can be used to find information in books. As a group, find references to 'The Plough' in the contents and index pages of one of the books. Look at each of the pages listed to find out more about the constellation and to see pictures of it. Give each child a piece of paper with the name of a constellation on it and an alphabet strip. Help the children to use the contents and index pages in the books to find a picture of the constellation on their piece of paper. If the children are unsure of where the initial of their constellation is in the alphabet, help them to look for it on the alphabet strip and then to use this to match with the letters on the index pages.

Supervise the children carefully and help them to copy the picture of their constellation onto the black paper by pricking it with a pin to mark the positions of each of the stars. Place a sheet of polystyrene underneath the paper first to protect the table-top.

Finally, label each constellation and tape them to a bright window so that the light can shine through the holes.

Support
Provide simple non-fiction books and let the children work in pairs.

Extension
Tell the children the name of a constellation. Help them to decide what the first letter of each constellation is from its initial sound.

Learning objective
To understand how information can be found in non-fiction texts.

Group size
Small group.

Home links
Ask parents and carers to share non-fiction books with their children and to use the contents and index pages.

Windy weather

Learning objective
To write to give information to the reader and to sequence events.

Group size
Small group.

What you need
A windy day; an information book showing the Beaufort scale; white A3 paper; drawing and writing materials; flip chart.

What to do
On a windy day, take the children outside or look together out of the window. Ask them to tell you how they know that it is windy. Encourage them to look for things that are moving or being blown. The children might see rubbish blowing along the road, tree branches swaying, or coats and scarves flapping about.

Write the children's observations on a flip chart. Show them the Beaufort scale and explain that it is a way of telling people, such as sailors, how strong the wind is. Tell the children that you would like them to make their own Beaufort scale. Using the observations that you wrote on the flip chart, help the children to decide which type of wind was the lightest, perhaps blowing paper around, and which was the strongest, maybe bending trees.

Sequence all the remaining comments about the wind in between the lightest and the strongest types of wind. You may want to give each type of wind a rating number.

Give each child a sheet of white A3 paper and ask them to draw a picture of one of the different strengths of wind. Provide help to the children with scribing an appropriate caption underneath each picture.

Make a weather-forecasting display with a selection of pictures showing different types of weather. Ideally, this could be close to an external door so the children can check the weather before they go outside. During each session, ask one child to say what they think the weather is like and then to select the picture that best describes it.

Support
Limit the amount of wind types that you use to make your Beaufort scale.

Extension
Ask the children to make individual copies of the wind scale.

Home links
Ask parents and carers to talk about the weather with their children. Encourage them to introduce different words and phrases that we use to describe the weather such as 'a shower' or 'raining cats and dogs' for rain, and 'scorching hot' or 'hazy' when it is sunny.

Spiders' webs

What you need
Information books about spiders and webs such as *Spiders* by Theresa Greenaway (*Minibeast Pets* series, Wayland); black or brown paper; string; drawing and writing materials; sheet of white card; small plate; scissors; stapler.

Preparation
Draw a spider shape onto the sheet of card. Use the small plate to make the body, add eight legs and a head and cut the spider out. Draw around the spider template on the black or brown paper several times (so that there is one spider for each child) and cut the spiders out.

What to do
Look at the information books about spiders with the children. Alternatively, take the children for a walk around the local area to search for spiders and their webs. (Misty, dewy mornings are a good time to do this. Look for the webs in hedgerows and gates or underneath window sills.)

Back at your setting, talk with the children about their observations of spiders and their webs. Encourage them to think about what spiders look like and what they do.

Give each child a paper spider and ask them to write their thoughts about spiders onto it. Encourage the children to 'sound out' the words as they write them and to make guesses at words that they are unsure about. Suggest to the children that they compare words that they do not know how to write with words and sounds that they are already familiar with.

Look together in the information books for pictures of webs. Decide on a size for a web that will be large enough for all of the children's spiders to fit on. Cut the string into lengths and help the children to tie the string together to make a web shape. Staple the spiders onto it.

Support
Help the children to write down just one idea about spiders. If necessary, act as a scribe, but ask the children to sound out the words to you as you write them.

Extension
Encourage the children to write more and to use reference books more independently.

Mr Pumpkin head

Learning objective
To retell a narrative in the correct sequence, drawing on the language patterns of stories.

Group size
Small group.

Home links
Explain the activity to parents and carers. Ask them to help their children to make a 'potato head' by gluing paper features onto a potato. Invite the children to bring in their potato heads and to tell the others how they made them.

What you need
The photocopiable sheet on page 73; pumpkin; newspaper; glue; spreaders; scissors; aprons; oddments of yellow wool; red, shiny material; uncooked macaroni; large, black buttons; grey, furry material; old black hat.

Preparation
Copy the photocopiable sheet and read through it several times to familiarize yourself with the story.

What to do
Tell the children that you are going to read them a story and that you would like to them to listen carefully. As you read the story, try to use a different voice for each character. At the end, talk with the children about the events in the story.

Show the children the pumpkin and explain that you would like them to make a 'pumpkin head', just like the children in the story. Ask the group if they can remember the first thing that was stuck onto the pumpkin. If the children have forgotten, re-read the appropriate part of the story. Ask the children to put on aprons and spread out the newspaper on a table. Help the children to retell the story by gluing the features onto the pumpkin in the same order in which they were added to the

pumpkin head in the story. Encourage them to try to remember and use the words that were said by each character.

If desired, the children could, either individually or as a group, make an illustrated list of instructions to tell someone else how to make a pumpkin head. Keep the instructions very pictorial and ask the children to include pictures of any materials needed. You may want to scribe the appropriate instructions by each picture. The children could also make up stories about the pumpkin head.

Support
Once the children have added a feature to the pumpkin, re-read the next part of the story to refresh the children's memories about what to glue onto the head next.

Extension
Encourage each child to make their own individual pumpkin head. Instead of using pumpkins, give the children paper plates to paint orange. When these are dry, the children can add the features.

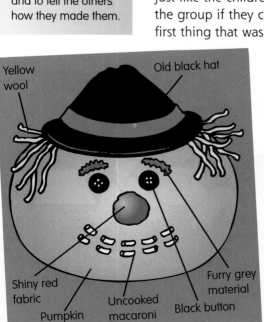

Yellow wool
Old black hat
Shiny red fabric
Pumpkin
Uncooked macaroni
Black button
Furry grey material

From leaf to leaf

What you need
Marker pen; 20 to 30 sheets of white A4 paper; scissors; large, open floor space.

Preparation
Draw a simple leaf shape on each sheet of A4 paper so that it almost fills the page, and cut the leaves out. Write in large letters in the middle of each leaf one word that the children will be able to read. For a topic on autumn or trees, you could use words such as 'oak', 'branch' or 'apple'.

What to do
Spread the leaves out across the large, open space like stepping-stones. Leave a gap of one leaf space between the leaves so that the children can step or jump across. Make sure that the words are facing upwards on each leaf.

Ask the children to spread out around the edge of the space and to stand on a leaf ready to start the game. On a given signal, ask them to cross from one side of the space to another by stepping on the leaves, reading out each leaf as they stand on it. As there is only room for one child on each leaf, encourage the children to look for leaves with no one stood on them. To vary the words, pick the leaves up in between games and ask the children to mix them up before spreading them out on the floor again.

Support
Keep the words short and simple, ensuring they are only made up of two or three letters, such as 'bag', 'sun' or 'hat'. Reduce the size of the empty space and use fewer leaves.

Extension
When writing on the leaves, choose words that begin with only three or four different letters such as 'c', 'r', 'b' and 'f'. Call out one of the initials and ask the children to stand only on leaves with words beginning with that letter.

Alternatively, make a list of sentences that could be made using the words on the leaves. Read out a sentence and ask individual children to find the words to spell out the sentence.

Learning objective
To read a range of familiar and common words independently.

Group size
Small group.

Home links
Write out two or three sentences onto thin card that contain some of the words on the leaves. Cut around each word and ask parents and carers to help their children to sequence the words and remake the sentences.

Foggy day

What you need
Large cardboard box; four or five large objects that the children will be able to recognize and name and which will fit inside the cardboard box, such as a teddy from the role-play area, a piece of dried wood or a large key; large sheet of greaseproof paper; sticky tape; foggy or misty day; scissors; paper; pen; torch.

Preparation
Open both cut ends of the box to make a 'tunnel'. Cover one end of the tunnel with the greaseproof paper and tape along one edge only. Make a list of words that the children may not know to describe the objects that you chose.

What to do
On a foggy or misty day, invite the children to look out of the window and tell you what they can see. Talk about how it is hard to see clearly in fog and mist. Explain that they are going to play a game where everything looks foggy!

Without the children seeing, hide one of the objects from the box just behind the greaseproof-paper screen. Tell the children what you have done and ask them to describe what they can see behind the paper. Encourage the children to use as many different words as possible. If the children find it hard to see the item, shine a torch on the back of the paper from the open end of the box.

Provide clues about the identity of the object, if necessary, using the list of words that you wrote down. Put each clue in a sentence to give the children a context for the meaning of the word. Encourage the children to ask for the meanings of any words that they are unsure about. Show the

children the item once they have guessed what it is. Continue with the remaining objects.

Support
Provide fewer objects and let the children touch the item by closing their eyes, lifting up the paper and putting their hand in the box.

Extension
Ask the children to describe the object without repeating a word that someone else has already said.

I'm sorry!

What you need
Just the children.

What to do
Ask the children to sit in a circle. Tell them that Yom Kippur is a Jewish festival that marks the final day of ten days of repentance. People apologize for anything that they should not have done to others or to God.

Talk with the children about things that are wrong or things that they wish they had not done. Ideas could include hitting a younger brother or sister, breaking another child's toy or not tidying up when they have been asked to. Discuss with the children how they feel when they have upset someone. Some of the children may say that they feel sorry. Encourage individual children to tell you about things that they feel they should not have done and what they should have done instead.

Begin the game by saying your name and something that you are sorry about, for example, 'I'm Mrs Lewis and I'm sorry that I shouted earlier'. Continue around the circle, letting each child in turn say something that they are sorry for. If some of the children cannot think of anything to say, encourage them to think of something that makes them feel sad, such as cruelty to animals or people dropping litter. Initially, some of the group may repeat what other children have already said.

The game finishes when everyone has had a turn at saying 'sorry'.

Extend the game by choosing a different emotion, such as happiness or anger, and encourage the children to describe something that makes them feel that emotion.

Support
Instead of asking children individually, talk as a group about things that the children could be sorry about. Encourage everybody to try to join in the conversation, even if the children are just agreeing with someone else.

Extension
Encourage the children to think of why they are sorry for what they have done wrong – perhaps they hurt someone's feelings, or maybe the toy they broke could not be repaired and so it cannot be played with any more.

Learning objective
To interact with
others, negotiating
plans and taking
turns in conversation.

Group size
Small group.

Travel to the moon

What you need
The story of the Chinese Moon Festival
and Chang Er – the spelling varies and
is sometimes written as Chang O or
Sheung Ngao – such as in *Faiths and
Festivals* by Martin Palmer (Ward Lock
Educational); white A3
paper; drawing and
writing materials; safety
scissors; glue stick; old
magazines with pictures of
vehicles and their
components.

Preparation
Read through the story of
the Chinese Moon Festival
several times to familiarize
yourself with it.

What to do
Read the story of the
Chinese Moon Festival to
the children and
encourage them to talk
about it, prompting them
with questions. Ask them
to think about how Chang
Er might have travelled to
the moon and invite them
to tell you what they know about space
travel and rockets.

Explain to the children that, as a
group, you would like them to design a
vehicle to get Chang Er to the moon.
Give each child a magazine and a pair
of scissors. Ask them to look through
the magazines and to cut out as many
pictures as possible that show parts of
vehicles (wheels, seats and so on). You
may want to give the children a time
limit for this.

Once everyone has finished, let the
children take it in turns to show the rest
of the group the pictures that they have
found. Encourage the children to look
at the pictures and to choose the parts
that they like best to turn into a picture

of something to take Chang Er to the
moon. Invite them to take turns in the
conversations and to listen to each
other's opinions.

Help the children to choose one
person to glue all the chosen parts
down on a large sheet of paper to
make a picture of the space vehicle.

Support
Cut two or three pictures of each type
of vehicle component from the
magazines and sort them into groups.
Ask the children to choose one
component at a time and to discuss
which one they want to use in their
group design.

Extension
Encourage the children to draw their
design first and then to choose, as a
group, the features that they like on
the individual designs to add to the
group picture.

Home links
Ask parents and
carers to include the
children in planning
and decision-making
such as what they are
going wear or what
they will have to eat.

Kiwi or aubergine

What you need

A selection of unusual fruit and vegetables; role-play table, chairs, cutlery and plates.

Preparation

Two or three days before you intend to carry out the activity, ask parents and carers to let their children bring in one piece of whole fresh fruit or vegetable (preferably something unusual or exotic) and its name written on a piece of paper.

What to do

Explain to the children that Sukkot is a Jewish festival that celebrates both the harvest and the time when the Jews wandered the deserts living in temporary shelters. The festival gives its name to a shelter (tabernacle) which is built just for Sukkot and where families eat and sleep. Traditionally, the Sukkot is decorated with an etrog (a yellow citrus fruit that is native to Israel) and tree branches – palms (lulav), myrtle (hadas) and willow (aravah). Other fruit and vegetables are also used to decorate the inside of the Sukkot.

Ask the children to sit in a circle with everyone holding the fruit or vegetable that they brought in from home and its label. Invite each child in turn to hold up their fruit or vegetable and to tell everyone what it is. If any of the children have forgotten what they have, help them to read the label.

Display the fruit and vegetables, with their labels, in the role-play area. Add a table and chairs, cutlery and plates so the children can pretend that they are eating in a Sukkot. Encourage the children to use the names of the fruit and vegetables in their role-play.

Support

Instead of asking each child to bring from home a piece of fruit and a label, provide a selection of five or six unusual fruit or vegetables to introduce to the children.

Extension

Give each child a paper bag with their name on it and ask them to put their fruit or vegetables in it. Let the children take it in turns to describe their fruit or vegetable for the rest of the group to guess what it is. The fruit can be taken out of the bag once someone has guessed correctly.

The farmer sows the seed

What you need
Yellow, green and brown sheets of
paper; information books about
farming and harvesting such as *Sowing
and Harvesting* by Ruth Versfeld (Oxfam
Educational); clothes that a farmer
might wear such as wellington boots,
hat, scarf and an overcoat; empty seed
packets; child-sized garden implements
such as spades, hoes and forks; baskets
for collecting produce; 'pretend' fruit
and vegetables or plastic flowers and
plants glued into plant pots; sticky tape.

Preparation
Tape yellow, green and brown sheets of
paper to the floor to restrict the size of
the area allowed for the different
sections of role-play.

What to do
Explain to the children that autumn is
traditionally the time when crops of
fruit and vegetables are picked or
gathered and harvested. Look together
at the information books about farming
and harvesting that you have collected
and talk with the children about the
jobs that farmers have to do to prepare
the crops and harvest them. Look for
pictures of the tools that farmers use
and the different harvesting techniques.

Ask the children to work in pairs to
plant, tend and harvest some of the
'pretend' fruit and vegetables or the
crops of the plastic flowers and plants in
pots. Let everyone 'plant' the fields,
'tend' them and 'harvest' them at the
same time, or rotate the jobs so that
one child is planting seeds while
another is watering a growing crop and
someone else is pretending to be the
farmer who is harvesting the fruit and
vegetables. Encourage the children to
use appropriate vocabulary for the
farming and harvesting, such as 'plant',
'harvest' or 'water', and to re-
enact some of the events that
they have read about in the
information books.

Extend the role-play by
making a farmhouse in one
corner of the role-play area or
paint a large cardboard box
red to make a combine
harvester. If possible, take the
group to visit a working farm
or a 'pick your own' centre
where the children can see
crops being harvested.

Support
Give the children set tasks to
re-enact, such as 'plant two
types of vegetable' or 'pick
the apples'.

Extension
Help the children to think of
ways that the role-play could
be extended.

Who will win?

What you need
The photocopiable sheet on page 74; dice; 'token' that the children can play for, such as a small counter; 26 small cards (playing card size is ideal).

Preparation
Copy the photocopiable sheet. Write one letter of the alphabet in lower case on each of the small cards.

What to do
Before the game, briefly introduce the festival of Navaratri to the children by explaining that it celebrates the victory of Rama over Ravana after nine days and nights of fighting. Show the children the photocopiable sheet. Place the counter in the middle of the 'board'. Explain that they are going to play a game to decide who will 'win' the counter by moving it back to the square next to their name.

Shuffle the alphabet cards and place them face down next to the board where both players can easily reach them. Let the children decide who will be Rama and who will be Ravana. The game begins with both players throwing the dice. The child who rolls the highest number starts first by taking an alphabet card and reading it. If the child knows the letter, they throw the dice. On a '1', '2' or '3', the player can move the counter that number of squares towards themselves. On a roll of '4', '5' or '6', the counter must be moved one square towards the other player. If the child cannot read the letter, the counter is not moved. The other player then takes an alphabet card and tries to read it, throws the dice if they have read correctly, and moves the counter according to the rules above. The game ends when the counter has been moved into the square next to Rama or Ravana.

Support
Give the children a smaller selection of letters. If necessary, provide clues to the letter by suggesting words beginning with that letter.

Extension
Make another set of letter cards to use in the game but written in upper case.

Puppet show

Learning objective
To show an understanding of the elements of stories, including the main character.

Group size
Small group.

What you need
White A4 card; thin canes or dowels; sticky tape; felt-tipped pens; the story of Rama and Sita from the Ramayana, for example, *Rama, the Heroic Prince* by Michelle Esclapex (*Tales of Heaven and Earth* series, Moonlight Publishing); scissors; table; large cloth to completely cover the table.

Preparation
Read through the story of Rama and Sita several times to familiarize yourself with it. You may also want to make a sample puppet.

What to do
Explain to the children that the story of Rama and Sita is often told during the Hindu festival of Divali. Read the story to the children and show them the pictures, talking about the sequence of events. Tell the children that you would like them to make puppets of the characters in the Ramayana, which can then be used to retell the story of Rama and Sita.

Give each child a piece of white card and some felt-tipped pens. Invite the children to choose one character from the story and to draw a picture of that person onto the card, adding colour with the felt-tipped pens.

Provide help to each child with cutting around the character they have drawn and with taping a cane or dowel onto the back of the card so that most of the cane is showing at the bottom of the puppet.

Remind the children of some of the main events in the Ramayana. Drape the large piece of cloth over the table and invite the children to sit behind it and to hold their puppets by the stick handles so that they can be seen above the table-top. Encourage the children to retell the story of the Ramayana, using as many of the words they heard from your reading as possible and concentrating on the actions of Rama. (If preferred, half of the group could retell the story while the other half watch. Then ask the children to swap roles.)

Support
Invite the children to sit in a group without the table. Re-read the story to them, pausing for them to hold up the appropriate puppet when each character name is mentioned.

Extension
Provide less intervention during the children's story retelling. Alternatively, encourage the children to think about what other characters did in the story, for example, Hanuman.

Home links
Ask parents and carers to tell stories to their children and to encourage them to retell favourite stories to other family members or a favourite soft toy.

Pop, screech, whoosh!

Learning objective
To hear and say initial and final sounds in words, and short vowel sounds within words.

Group size
Small group.

What you need
Felt-tipped pens; the photocopiable sheet on page 75; flip chart.

Preparation
Make a copy the photocopiable sheet for each child.

What to do
Explain to the children that you are going to say some noises that they might hear on Bonfire Night. Give each child a copy of the photocopiable sheet and read through the words together. Re-read each word slowly. Ask each child in turn to repeat one word and to say what sound they think the word begins with. Once the children are confident at this, ask them to say what sound they think each of the words ends with. Finally, help the children as a group to decide and say what sounds the words have in the middle of them. If necessary, use the felt-tipped pens to highlight each part of the words.

Ask the children to take it in turns to say a word, and encourage the rest of the group to say the sound that the word starts with, ends with or has in its middle.

Make this a regular activity by choosing one word each week and displaying it in your setting. As a group, read the word and say what each of the component sounds is. Alternatively, choose a sound and write as many words as possible which contain that sound on a flip chart. Start with a sound that could be used as the beginning of a word, such as 'sh'.

Support
Invite the children to say just the initial sound of each word.

Extension
Put the children into groups of three. Give each group a word that they can read. Ask one child to say the initial sound, another to say the middle sound and the last child to say the ending sound. Challenge the children to read the word with each child saying the appropriate sound in the correct order.

Home links
Ask parents and carers to read and sing books and stories which include sounds with their children, such as 'Old Macdonald Had a Farm'. Encourage them to help their children to decide what sound each of the noises begins with, for example, 'woof' begins with 'w'.

Make a dreidel

What you need
Drawing and writing materials; the photocopiable sheet on page 76; sheets of white A4 card; safety scissors; glue; spreaders; sharpened pencils.

Preparation
Copy the photocopiable sheet onto card for each child plus two or three extra copies. Cut out the dreidel from one of the extra copies and write a letter on each blank face. Carefully glue the flaps on the sides of the dreidel and stick the sides together with the letters on the outside. Make a hole at the top and carefully push the sharpened end of the pencil through the hole so that the point of the pencil is at the end of the dreidel. Make sure that at least five centimetres of the blunt end of the pencil are still visible at the top of the dreidel. Make holes for a pencil on all the remaining copies.

What to do
Explain to the children that Jewish children play with dreidels at Hanukkah. Show them the dreidel that you have made and say that,

traditionally, dreidels have Hebrew letters written on them. Explain to the children that you would like them to make their own dreidels, but to decorate them with alphabet letters instead of Hebrew ones.

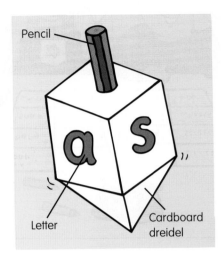

Pencil
Letter
Cardboard dreidel

Give each child a copy of the photocopiable sheet. Help them to carefully cut out the dreidels. Provide each child with a pencil or crayon to write a different letter, either upper or lower case, on each face of the dreidel that does not have a hole in it. Help the children to glue the dreidels together, then leave these to dry.

Push a pencil through the holes in each of the dreidels for the children. Ask them to take turns to spin their dreidels by twisting the pencil. Which letter is uppermost when the dreidel stops spinning?

Support
Help the children with cutting and gluing. Give each child a card with their name written on it and ask them to copy a different letter from their name onto each face of the dreidel.

Extension
Encourage the children to write letter combinations onto each face of the dreidel, such as 'bl' or 'dr'.

Dress the bear

What you need
The photocopiable sheets on pages 77 and 78; table; scissors; sticky-backed plastic (optional).

Preparation
Enlarge both of the photocopiable sheets onto thin A3 card for each child and for demonstration. Cut out the bears, labels and items of clothing. If desired, laminate the pictures and labels.

What to do
Show the children the bear and explain that you would like them to put some clothes on it. Put two or three of the clothes labels and some of the clothing pictures in the middle of the table. Help the children to read the words, find the clothing that matches each label and dress the bear in the clothes.

Give each child a bear and two or three labels with different combinations of words. Put all the clothing pictures in the middle of the table and encourage the children to read the words, find the clothes to match these and then dress the bear.

Vary the activity by drawing other items of clothing such as seasonal wear, for example, shorts, T-shirts and sunglasses. Alternatively, make pictures and labels for clothes from other cultures such as a kimono, sari or shalwar kameez.

Support
Give each child one label to try to read. Encourage the children to look at the initial letter and the overall shape of the word.

Extension
Glue plain paper over the pictures and labels on the photocopiable sheets and re-photocopy the bear and the blank squares. Ask the children to look through old mail order catalogues and to cut out items of clothing with their appropriate labels. Provide help to the children with gluing the pictures and labels in each of the spaces on the photocopied sheets and with cutting them out. Ask the children to work in pairs to read each other's labels and find the correct clothing for the bear.

Learning objective:
To read a range of familiar and common words.

Group size
Small group.

Home links
Ask parents and carers to encourage their children to read signs and labels when they are out shopping together. Ask them to write down and draw the clothes that they would like their children to put on one morning and then to help the children to read the list and select the appropriate items of clothing.

Jack Frost

What you need
A4 paper in shades of blue and grey; drawing and writing materials in shades of blue, grey, white and silver; large sheets of blue paper; glue; spreaders; scissors; materials for decorating in silvers, blues and greys such as glitter, gummed shapes, ribbon and wool; sticky tape; flip chart; display board; pins; a frosty day.

What to do
Invite the children to look out of the window on a frosty day and to tell you

what they can see. Draw the children's attention to signs of overnight freezing such as icicles, frozen puddles or hoar frost on the grass. Tell the children that, traditionally, Jack Frost walks around at night making ice and frost. Ask the children what they think Jack Frost might look like. Write the children's ideas down on a flip chart.

Tape some of the large blue sheets of paper together to make a big rectangle and draw on a child-sized outline of Jack Frost. Ask the children to help you add features and clothes to the outline. When the picture of Jack Frost is finished and the glue is dry, pin the picture to a display board.

Encourage each child to tell you something about Jack Frost and what he does. When they have thought of something to say, let them choose an A4 sheet of paper and a coloured pen or pencil and invite them to write their thoughts down on the paper in whatever way they can. Tell the children to keep their ideas brief and, if possible, to write a capital letter at the beginning of the thought and a full stop at the end. Remind the children to write their name at the end of their captions. Display the children's thoughts around the picture of Jack Frost on the display board.

Support
If necessary, scribe for the children and draw their attention to the punctuation as you are writing. Provide the children's name cards for them to copy.

Extension
Encourage the children to write longer captions and to make sure that they have used capital letters for the first letters of their names.

Learning objective
To write their own names, labels and captions, sometimes using punctuation.

Group size
Small group.

Home links
Ask parents and carers to help their children to name and label any pictures that they draw or paint at home.

Snow and snowflakes

What you need
Pictures and books showing snow and snowflakes such as *Snow* by Miranda Ashwell (*What is Weather?* series, Heinemann); safety scissors; white paper discs (10cm in diameter); sheets of brightly coloured card; glue sticks; black writing materials.

snow is cold
snow is pretty
snow is white

What to do
Give each child a white paper disc and a pair of safety scissors. Help them to fold their circles in half, the straight edge at the bottom, and curl both of the 'corners' up to the top of the curved edge of the semicircle to make a cone shape. With the disc still folded, help them to cut out small triangles from the folds. Make sure that the children do not cut right across the folded disc.

Ask the children to carefully unfold their papers to reveal a snowflake shape. Invite them to choose a sheet of brightly coloured card and help them to glue their snowflakes in the middle of their sheets of card.

Encourage the children to tell you everything that they know about snow, such as what it looks like, what it feels like and what you can do with it. Look together at the pictures and books showing snow and snowflakes.

Explain to the children that you would like them to write a simple poem about snow, such as 'I like snow because…, I like snow because…'.

Give each child a black pen and ask them to write their ideas across the snowflake that they glued to the card. Encourage the children to write each new thought on a new line. Invite them to read each other's poems when they have finished.

Support
Keep the poems very simple, perhaps asking the children just to make a list of words that could be used to describe snow. The children could also work together on a group poem. If necessary, scribe the children's poems for them.

Extension
Encourage the children to write longer poems and to begin to use punctuation and rhymes in their poems.

Learning objective
To make up their own poems.

Group size
Small group.

Home links
Ask parents and carers to read rhymes and poems to their children. Make a list of recommended books that include rhymes and poems, such as *Poems for the Very Young* by Michael Rosen (Kingfisher Books). Alternatively, laminate copies of the children's poems and let them borrow each other's work to read at home with their parents or carers.

Fold the circle in half to make a semicircle.

Cut small triangles from the folds on the folded circle.

Fold both of the corners of the straight edge of the semicircle upwards to meet the curved edge of the semicircle and make a cone shape.

Tracks in the snow

What you need
The photocopiable sheet on page 79; sheets of white A4 paper and pencils (or pale-coloured sugar paper and charcoal); books about animal tracks such as *Whose Tracks Are These?* by James Nail (Roberts Rinehart).

Preparation
Read through the story on the photocopiable sheet several times to familiarize yourself with it.

What to do
Give each child a sheet of white A4 paper and a pencil (or a piece of sugar paper and a stick of charcoal). Explain that you are going to read them a story and that you would like them to listen very carefully to it. Continue by saying that at certain points in the story you will ask them to draw something on their sheet of paper.

Read the story to the children using different voices for each character and as much expression as possible. At suitable points, stop reading and ask the children to draw something on their sheet of paper, for example, a snowman, a tree, an animal track or one of the animals mentioned. While

the children are drawing, they could also talk about what they have heard so far and try to predict what they think will happen next.

Encourage the children to ask questions about anything that they are uncertain about as they are listening to you or drawing. Throughout the reading, make sure that they are continuing to listen. When you have finished reading the story, invite the children to retell it to each other or record it onto a cassette recorder using a microphone.

Alternatively, draw pictures of each of the animal tracks or read more about animal tracks by using reference books about animals.

Support
Pause more frequently when reading the story and encourage the children to talk about what has happened up to that point.

Extension
Read the story all the way through without stopping, except for the children to make predictions. Encourage them to comment on the story at the end of the reading.

Feed the birds

What you need
Rectangular box; red paper; glue; spreaders; scissors; paper; writing materials; envelopes; greetings stamps; non-fiction books about looking after birds in winter.

Preparation
Make sure that all ends of the box are sealed, and stand it on one of its small ends. Cut a slot in one of the long sides a quarter of the way down from the top. Cover the box with the red paper, leaving the slot open to make a post-box. Cut a large hole in the back of the box, opposite the slot, so that the mail can be collected. Make a sign saying, 'Collection times: 1. Midday'.

What to do
Explain to the children that you would like them to put some food out for the birds in the winter, but you do not know what they should eat. Say that you would like them to write a letter to someone who might know what birds like to eat in winter. Encourage the children to think of people who might know, such as a vet or a pet shop owner.

Give each child a sheet of paper to write their letter on. Talk with the children about the format of letters such as where they should write their address, 'Dear Sir' and 'Yours faithfully'. Help the children to write a letter to their chosen person asking what sort of food birds like to eat in winter. When the letters are finished, ask the children to seal them in an envelope, add a stamp and put them in the post-box.

Use the reference books or talk to a vet or pet shop owner to find out what birds eat in winter. Write a reply to each of the children's letters and put them in the post-box. Next session, ask one of the children to empty the post-box and deliver the letters. Help the children to read their letters.

Support
Give the children a template to fill in which includes the address of your setting, 'Dear Sir', and 'Yours faithfully'. Scribe for the children if necessary.

Extension
Encourage the children to write more independently and to use simple dictionaries to check their spellings.

Learning objective
To write a letter using features of letter-writing.

Group size
Small group.

Slot for letters

Box covered with red paper

Home links
Ask parents and carers to provide opportunities for their children to write letters at home, such as inviting a favourite toy to a tea party.

Winter plants

What you need
Information books about evergreen plants found in winter, such as *British Trees* by Angela Royston (*Plants* series, Heinemann); A4 white paper; black marker pen; word processor and printer (if available); scissors.

Preparation
Using the information books, make a list of plants that can be seen in winter such as pine trees, mistletoe, holly and ivy. Write a brief description about each plant including what it looks like, where it can be found or any traditions associated with it. Try to use only words that the children will be able to read. Copy your ideas in large print on an A4 sheet of paper or type them on a word processor using a font size of 36 or 48. Photocopy or print out the sheet for each child.

What to do
Read through the plant descriptions together with the children. Help them to sound out any words that they are unsure about and talk with them about the meanings of any words that they do not know. Show them the pictures of each of the plants in the books.

Explain to the children that you would like them to cut out the words and rearrange these to make new descriptions. Give them a time limit, such as five minutes, to cut out the words and mix them up into new sentences. If necessary, help the children to carefully cut around each word. Invite them to take it in turns to read out loud the new descriptions. Some may be completely nonsensical. Repeat for as long as desired.

Support
Make shorter descriptions for the children, perhaps just one sentence per plant with as few words as possible.

Extension
Challenge the children to use as many of the words as possible to write new descriptions which still make sense when you read them.

Alternatively, ask the children to carefully cut each word in half vertically and then to mix and match each of the word endings.

On the first of December

What you need
Two large pieces of A1 card; drawing and writing materials; scissors; pencil.

Preparation
Draw 24 identical rectangles onto one sheet of card. Copy the exact positions of each of the rectangles onto the other piece of card. On one piece of card, write a different word in each rectangle that the children can read. Words could be linked to a theme such as 'clothes', 'food' or 'Christmas'.

On the other sheet of card, draw a picture of a Christmas-related object, almost filling the piece of card – for example, Father Christmas, a star or a Christmas tree. On this piece of card, cut carefully around each rectangle to make 24 doors, leaving the left-hand side of each rectangle uncut. Write a number from 1 to 24 randomly on the outside of each of the doors. Glue the picture face up onto the sheet where you wrote the words so that these can be easily seen through each of the doors. Close all the doors.

What to do
Tell the children that Advent Sunday marks the start of the Advent period. Explain that many Christians count down the days to Christmas by opening one door each day on an Advent calendar beginning on the first day of December.

Show the children the calendar that you have made. Explain that there is one door for each of the days leading up to Christmas and that behind each door is a word. Explain to the children that each day you will choose one child to open the next door on the calendar and read the word behind it. Begin with the door labelled '1'; on the following day, open the door marked '2', then door '3' the next day, and so on until the last day before the Christmas holidays, when you can let the children open any doors that have not been opened. Make sure that each child has a turn at opening a door.

Support
Write shorter, more familiar words in the rectangles.

Extension
Write longer, more unusual words in the rectangles. Encourage the children to check the meanings of any new words in dictionaries.

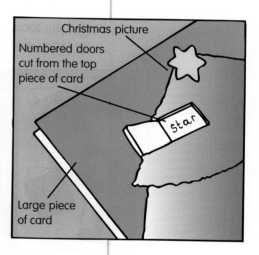

Christmas picture

Numbered doors cut from the top piece of card

Large piece of card

star

Learning objective
To read a range of familiar and common words independently.

Group size
Large or small group.

Home links
Ask parents and carers to help their children to find and use one new word each day during the days before Christmas (or another seasonal festival).

Dear Father Christmas

What you need
The photocopiable sheet on page 80;
sheets of white A4 paper; marker pen;
drawing and writing materials.

Preparation
Draw a large arrow on two sheets of A4
paper and label them 'right' or 'left' as
appropriate. Read through the letter on
the photocopiable sheet several times
to familiarize yourself with it.

What to do
Ask the children if they have ever
written letters to Father Christmas. Talk
with them about how they think Father
Christmas delivers the presents. How do
Father Christmas and the reindeers
manage to find everyone's house? Do
the children think it is magic, or does
Father Christmas have a map?

Explain to the children that you are
going to read a letter that was written to
Father Christmas by a little boy to make

sure that Father Christmas found the
right house to deliver the presents to.

Ask the children to listen carefully as
you read the letter on the
photocopiable sheet to them. Talk with
the group about some of the directions
that were mentioned in the letter.
Check that the children know which way
is left and which is right.

Tell the children that you would like
them to think about how they could
direct Father Christmas
from the North Pole to
their house. Talk
together about some of
the landmarks that
Father Christmas could
look out for such as
churches and other tall
buildings, road names or
distinctive objects such
as odd-looking trees and
duck ponds.

Ask each child to
explain to the others
how they would direct
Father Christmas to their
house. Help the children
to write their ideas onto
a piece of paper using
the arrows that you drew
as a guide, together with
illustrations. Encourage
the children to read each
other's directions.

Support
Help the children to work together as a
group to make verbal instructions that
would guide Father Christmas to each
of their houses.

Extension
Invite the children to look at large-
scale maps of your local area and
encourage them to find street names
and check directions. Trace a route from
your setting to the park, for example.

Money, money, money

What you need

Examples of real English or foreign banknotes, or books showing pictures of money, such as *Money* by Joe Cribb (*Eyewitness Guide* series, Dorling Kindersley); several pieces of white paper (approximately 15cm x 8cm); drawing and writing materials.

What to do

Explain to the children that Eid-ul-Fitr is celebrated at the end of the fast of Ramadan. During this festival, Muslims give away money to people worse off than themselves.

Show the children the banknotes or look together at the pictures of money in the books. Talk with the children about the features that you usually find on banknotes, such as the head of a king or queen, a picture of a famous person and the dates when they lived and died, or a number showing the value of the note. Tell the children that you would like them to make their own banknotes.

Give each child a piece of white paper and a pencil. Encourage them to design their note first and decide where they are going to put the pictures and writing. Remind the group that banknotes have pictures and writing on both sides of the paper. Once the children have drafted their banknotes, give them another sheet of paper so that they can draw their note again, this time using colour. Encourage the children to hold their pencil correctly and to carefully write out each of the letters and numbers.

Laminate copies of the children's notes and create a shop in the role-play area where the children can spend their money. Remind the group that their money cannot be used in real shops.

Support

Ask the children to write on one side of the paper only. Provide reference sheets with numbers from one to ten and the alphabet written on.

Extension

Encourage the children to add more writing to the banknotes and to use higher numbers.

New Year resolutions

What you need
An A4 scrapbook or similar-sized blank book; drawing and writing materials; sheets of different-coloured A4 paper.

Preparation
Make a list of some possible New Year resolutions such as 'I will read everyday' or 'I will stop biting my nails'.

What to do
Begin by explaining to the children that New Year is a time for new beginnings and a fresh start, and that some people like to make 'New Year resolutions' at the beginning of a new year. Explain that these are things that people would like to do, or would like to stop doing, and that usually they are something good. Tell the children the examples of New Year resolutions on your list.

Ask each child to think of something that they could do as a New Year's resolution and to tell the rest of the group what it would be. Ideas might include not hitting a younger sister or learning to ride a bike. Invite each child to choose a sheet of paper and some drawing and writing materials. Ask them to draw their New Year's resolution and to add a suitable caption in their own level of writing but emphasize that they should write from left to right and top to bottom. Once the resolutions are finished, glue all the work in the scrapbook and add a suitable title to the front of the book. Read the book together as a group, or let the children take it in turns to read each other's resolutions.

Support
Encourage the children to keep their resolutions short. Act as a scribe for the children, if necessary, but ask them where you should start writing on the paper, and where you should start writing again at the end of each line.

Extension
Encourage the children to begin to use simple punctuation when writing their New Year's resolutions such as capital letters and full stops.

Pass the seaweed, please

What you need
Ten paper plates; pictures of food cut from magazines or pretend food, including examples of Japanese food such as sushi, seaweed, bamboo shoots and rice; glue; sticky tape.

Preparation
Glue the pictures of food or tape the pretend food to the paper plates.

What to do
Explain to the children that Ganjitsu is New Year's Day in Japan and that, traditionally, it is a time for families to join together and eat a soup called 'zoni', made with rice, fish and vegetables.

Ask the children to sit in a large circle on the floor facing into the centre. Show the children the plates of pictures or pretend food and talk about the contents of each plate. Make sure that everyone knows what is on each plate.

Put all the plates in the centre of the circle and tell the children that you would like them to take turns to pass each other plates of food. Begin the game yourself by saying, for example, 'Please, Ben, could you pass me the plate with the seaweed on?'. Once the food has been passed, say 'Thank you, Ben'. Put the plate back in the centre of the circle and then ask the child who passed you a plate to choose another person in the circle to pass them a plate, speaking clearly and slowly, and

remembering to say 'please' and 'thank you' at appropriate times. Continue with the children taking turns to ask each other for something until everyone in the circle has had the opportunity to ask for something and give thanks.

Support
Use three plates of food and put each type of food onto a different-coloured plate to make it easier for the children to remember what the contents of each plate are.

Extension
Provide a selection of pretend food where each plate has items that all begin with the same initial letter, for example, a 'p' plate with peas, plums and pears, an 'r' plate with rice, radish and raspberries, and an 's' plate with sushi, sausages and sauerkraut.

Learning objective
To speak clearly and audibly with confidence and use conventions such as 'please' and 'thank you'.

Group size
Large or small group.

Home links
Ask parents and carers to have a 'polite day' at home when all the family tries to remember to say 'please' and 'thank you'.

As easy as abc

What you need
Small chalkboards and white or multicoloured chalks, or small whiteboards and markers.

What to do
Explain to the children that Saraswati Puja celebrates Saraswati, the Hindu goddess of learning and that, traditionally, Hindu children start school during this festival. The alphabet is one of the first things that the children learn about.

Divide the children into pairs and give each child a chalkboard and a selection of chalks or a whiteboard and markers. Ask the pairs of children to decide who will be the 'teacher' and who will be the 'pupil'.

Explain that you would like each of the 'teachers' to ask the 'pupils' to write some letters on their boards. Initially, the 'teachers' should ask the 'pupils' to write one letter at a time, which the 'teacher' can then check to see if it is correct. When the children have done this, ask the 'teachers' to name three or four letters for the 'pupils' to write. If the 'teachers' forget the letters they asked for, encourage them to write them on their board as they say them so that they can refer back to them later.

Once the 'pupil' has finished writing, ask them to read out each of the letters that they wrote, pointing at them in turn. Ask the 'teacher' to check the answers. Encourage the 'teachers' to be as positive as possible about the answers, especially if some of the letters are not the ones that were asked for or are not well formed. Let the children swap roles.

Alternatively, give each 'teacher' a card with each of the letters of the alphabet on. Ask them to point to a letter, but not say what it is, for the 'pupil' to name and copy.

Support
Give each pair of children an identical set of magnetic or card letters. Ask the 'teachers' to name a letter for their 'pupils' to find.

Extension
Ask the 'teachers' to suggest combinations of letters for the 'pupils' to write, such as 'tr' or 'ing'.

Happy New Year

What you need

Red A4 card; gold wax crayons; thin white paper; plastic money in a variety of sizes and denominations; black and gold felt-tipped pens; scissors; examples of Chinese New Year cards; glue sticks.

Preparation

Fold each sheet of A4 card in half to make an A5 card.

What to do

Show the children your collection of Chinese New Year cards. Look together at the writing on the cards and explain to the children that you would like them to make their own New Year cards.

Give each child a piece of the white paper, a gold wax crayon and some of the plastic money, and invite them to put the money under the paper. Demonstrate to the children how to hold the coin in place and to colour over the top of the paper using the wax crayon to make a rubbing. Let each child do this several times and then help them to cut out the rubbings.

Give each child a folded card and remind them that the fold should be on the left-hand side of the card. Invite the children to glue their coin rubbings onto the front of their cards.

Explain to the children that they now need to add some writing to their card to tell other people what the card is celebrating. Discuss suitable messages for Chinese New Year that the children could add inside their cards, for

example, 'Best wishes for the New Year' or 'Wishing you luck and happiness in the New Year'.

Invite the children to write 'Happy New Year' on the front of their cards and to scribe an appropriate message inside. Encourage them to use sentences rather than just words. They

could also, with your help, draw Chinese-style characters.

Support

Write the sentences and captions for the children to copy.

Extension

Encourage the children to write longer captions and to begin to use punctuation, especially capital letters on the first words and full points.

Learning objective
To listen with enjoyment to stories and songs and make up their own.

Group size
Small group to make the book; large or small group to sing the songs.

Home links
Ask parents and carers to sing with their children at home and to encourage them to experiment with and change the words in the songs.

Dance and sing

What you need
Plain white paper plates; drawing and writing materials; glue; materials to decorate the plates, such as feathers, sequins, glitter, scraps of paper and fabric; white A4 paper; computer with word-processing software and printer (optional); hole-punch; ribbon.

Preparation
Draw a face onto one of the paper plates and decorate it with some of the feathers, glitter and so on.

What to do
Tell the children that during Mardi Gras, people dress up and walk through the streets, dancing and singing to music. Ask the children which songs they like to sing. Explain that you would like them to each make up a song. Mardi Gras is a happy time, so encourage them to write about things that make them feel happy. Ideas could include playing with a brother or sister, going on holiday or wearing new clothes. If the children find it difficult to think of a tune, suggest that they fit some words to a favourite traditional tune such as 'Twinkle, Twinkle Little Star'. Alternatively, the children could mix up lines from existing songs and rhymes, for example, 'Humpty Dumpty sat on the wall, Incy Wincy Spider climbed up the spout, the mouse ran down the clock'. Provide help to the children with writing the songs or using a computer if necessary.

Give each child a paper plate and show them the one that you decorated. Invite them to draw a face on their

plate and to decorate it using the selection of materials. Staple the children's songs to the lower edge of each of their plates and encourage the children to read and sing the songs.

If desired, make the songs into a book by creating a hole at the top of each plate and threading them together with a piece of ribbon.

Support
Invite the children to make a group song and provide help to each child with scribing one line in the song. Make multiple copies so that each child can have a copy to sing from.

Extension
Encourage the children to work more independently.

Decorated paper plate

I like to dance
I like to sing
I like ice-cream
and holidays.

Children's song

Babies everywhere

Mrs Jones, the farmer, met Suzy, Rajan and Monique at the farm gate.

'Morning, Suzy, would you and your friends like to see some of our baby animals?'

'Yes, please,' replied Suzy.

'Let's look at the hens first then,' said Mrs Jones, 'follow me.'

Together, they squelched their way across the farmyard with their wellies sticking in the mud at every step. Near the farmhouse was a large pen covered in wire netting. In the middle of the pen there was a small wooden shed. Walking around inside the pen were two brown hens pecking at some grain on the floor. Mrs Jones opened a hatch in the netting. Inside the hen house were three tiny, fluffy, yellow birds.

'Do you know what baby hens are called?' asked the farmer.

'They're chicks,' said Rajan.

Mrs Jones reached into the coop and took out the chicks for the children to hold.

'What animal would you like to see next?' asked Mrs Jones.

'Do you have any pigs?' asked Monique, 'I think they're so sweet.'

They walked across the farmyard to a large shed. It was warm and smelled of straw. In the corner was a fat pink pig. Next to her were lying six tiny piglets.

After the pigsty, Mrs Jones led the children to some fields behind the farmhouse. From the first gate, the children could see some large animals resting in the grass. Some were black and white and some were brown.

'Cows!' said Suzy, 'I can't see any baby cows though.'

'Look! Over there. Near the trees. There's a calf with its mummy, and there's another calf by the fence,' cried Rajan.

Suzy pointed at a calf behind another cow too.

From the next field came the sound of bleating. 'It's so loud,' said Monique. Mrs Jones explained to the children that the baby sheep baa to find their mothers.

Rajan suddenly began laughing. 'That sheep can't stand up. It just fell over, and again.'

'That lamb was only born this morning, which is why it's so wobbly,' explained Mrs Jones.

A large blackbird landed on the ground next to one of the calves with a big worm in its beak.

'What a huge worm,' gasped Rajan.

'That's to feed the baby birds, isn't it?' asked Suzy.

'Mmm, that's right. I think there is a nest in the hedge over there. I haven't looked too closely though because I don't want to scare the birds or they won't come back again. I think that's all our new babies. Would you like to come back to the farmhouse for a big glass of milk each?' said Mrs Jones.

'Yes, please,' chorused the children.

Lorraine Gale

Robin Oliver yawned

v i b g y o r

Next was a plague of frogs

plague of blood

plague of frogs

plague of lice

plague of wild beasts

plague of sickness

plague of boils

plague of hail

plague of locusts

plague of darkness

plague of death

The gilip squibbled

A piplock teaser
Hold out your flibflobs
  and croodle your eyes.
In the blink of a muggit
  you'll get a surprise:

Smell its sweet pongle
  and harkle its grizz.
Feel its flumper and
  guess what it is.

Celia Warren

Sing a song of spligworth
Sing a song of spligworth
A pocket full of gry,
Twenty-seven gumbies
Blimped in a pie.
When the pie was pombled
The gumbies made a pish,
Now wasn't that a dainty splog
To flump before a fish!

Celia Warren

Minibeast rhymes

Five little woodlice

One little woodlouse living all alone,
One little woodlouse under a stone.

Two little woodlice eating a stick,
Two little woodlice under a brick.

Three little woodlice sleeping a while,
Three little woodlice under a tile.

Four little woodlice tightly packed,
Four little woodlice hiding in a crack.

Five little woodlice run away in shock,
Someone has found them under a rock.

Celia Warren

Minifeasts for minibeasts

Here's a web in which will hide a brown
and speckled eight-legged spider.
  If she waits she'll be the winner
  of a big fat fly for dinner.

Here's some soil in which will squirm
a wriggly, wiggly hungry worm.
  All day long he simply munches
  rotting leaves and soily lunches.

Here's a tree which is the filler
of a hungry caterpillar.
Underneath each little leaf
  she nibbles, silent as a thief.

Here's a warm and sunny sky,
  waiting for a butterfly...

Celia Warren

Summer sun shines on and on

(Tune: 'Bobby Shaftoe')

CHORUS
Summer sun shines on and on
Summer sun shines on and on
Summer sun shines on and on
Shines on all the birds.

1. Birds are singing in the sun
Birds are singing in the sun
Birds are singing in the sun
On and on and on.

CHORUS
Summer sun shines on and on...
Shines on all the bees.

2. Bees are buzzing in the sun...
On and on and on.

CHORUS
Summer sun shines on and on...
Shines on all the cats.

3. Cats are sleeping in the sun...
On and on and on.

CHORUS
Summer sun shines on and on...
Shines on all the ants.

4. Ants are working in the sun...
On and on and on.

CHORUS
Summer sun shines on and on...
Shines on everyone.

5. Friends are dancing in the sun...
On and on and on.

> Make up extra verses for sheep, cows, dogs, ducks, hens, trees and so on.
>
> Ask the children to stand in a circle with a space in between each child. Invite one child to be the leader who walks around the circle, weaving in and out of the other children while they sing the chorus. The leader then taps another child on the shoulder and together they move around the circle singing the verse. The leader then returns to his place in the circle and the person they chose becomes the new leader.

Ann Bryant

It's sunny

16 July	17 July Put on sunblock. Move on 2 squares.	18 July	19 July
23 July Find it hard to sleep. Move back 1 square.	22 July	21 July	20 July
24 July	25 July	26 July Have a cold drink. Move on 3 squares.	27 July
31 July	30 July Sports day. Move on 5 squares.	29 July	28 July
1 August Get sunburnt. Miss a turn.	2 August	3 August	4 August
8 August	7 August	6 August	5 August Wear new T-shirt. Move on 2 squares.
9 August	10 August	11 August Visit the beach. Miss a turn.	12 August
16 August	Put on sun-glasses. Move on 2 squares. 15 August	14 August	13 August
17 August Too hot. Miss a turn.	18 August	19 August	20 August
24 August	23 August Look for minibeasts. Move on 1 square.	22 August	21 August

 # It's raining

16 July	17 July	18 July	**19 July** Put on coat. Move on 3 squares.
23 July	**22 July** Forget hat. Move back 1 square.	21 July	20 July
24 July Borrow umbrella. Move on 3 squares.	25 July	26 July	27 July
31 July	**30 July** Have to stay inside. Miss a turn.	29 July	28 July
1 August	2 August	3 August	**4 August** Go to look for worms. Move on 1 square.
8 August	7 August	Travel on bus. Move on 5 squares **6 August**	5 August
9 August	**10 August** Step in a puddle. Move back 2 squares.	11 August	12 August
16 August	**15 August** Put on wellies. Move on 3 squares.	14 August	13 August
17 August	**18 August** Hole in shoe. Miss a turn.	19 August	20 August
24 August	23 August	22 August	21 August

Mr Pumpkin head

Akshar, Kyle, Jodie and Sacha were playing 'Snap' at the kitchen table with Mrs Singh.

The front door slammed.

'Hello', called Mr Singh. 'I'm home.'

Akshar jumped down from his chair and ran to meet his Dad.

'Can you take that big bag by the door into the kitchen, please?' said Mr Singh.

Akshar looked in the bag. In it was something round and orange. 'Dad? What's this?'

Mr Singh smiled. 'It's a pumpkin, I thought you and your friends could help me turn it into a head'.

'With magic?' gasped Sacha.

'Not quite', laughed Mr Singh. 'We'll need newspaper to put on the table, glue, scissors, and bits of wool and material.'

Mrs Singh went to fetch her sewing box. Kyle and Jodie spread some paper over the kitchen table. Soon there was a pile of old balls of wool and scraps of material heaped on the table.

'Every head needs a nose. What do you think would make a good nose for our pumpkin head?' asked Mr Singh.

'I like that red, shiny material,' pointed Jodie. 'Could we use that?'

'Who else likes that idea?' asked Akshar's father.

'The head would look good with a big red nose,' said Kyle.

Jodie cut out a circle from the red cloth.

'Glue it in the middle of the pumpkin, on the side,' suggested Mr Singh.

'Our head needs a mouth. Some macaroni would look just like teeth.' Akshar bared his teeth and growled. Sacha giggled. He got some pasta from the cupboard and carefully glued it in two rows under the pumpkin's nose.

'Mrs Singh,' said Kyle. 'Do you have any big black buttons in your sewing box, please? I want to use them to make the pumpkin's eyes.' Together they found two large black buttons and Kyle glued them onto the pumpkin.

Sacha saw some grey fluffy material in the pile of scraps on the table. 'I'm going to use this to make two eyebrows just like my Grandad's – all big and grey and bushy!'

'Our pumpkin hasn't got any hair,' said Jodie. 'Let's stick some wool on top of the pumpkin. I can see some yellow curly wool that looks a bit like hair.'

Mrs Singh helped Jodie cut the wool into lengths. Akshar smeared glue all over the top of the pumpkin. Everyone helped to stick handfuls of wool onto the glue.

Mr Singh walked out of the kitchen and went upstairs. He came back shortly holding a big black hat. 'Just the thing to finish off such a wonderful pumpkin head,' he grinned.

Lorraine Gale

EARLY YEARS AROUND THE YEAR Communication, language and literacy

Who will win?

1	2	3	4	5	6	7	8	9
9	8	7	6	5	4	3	2	1

Start

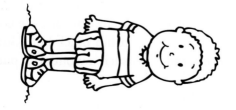

Pop, screech, whoosh!

pop

fizz

bang

screech

snap

whoosh

whistle

boom

Make a dreidel

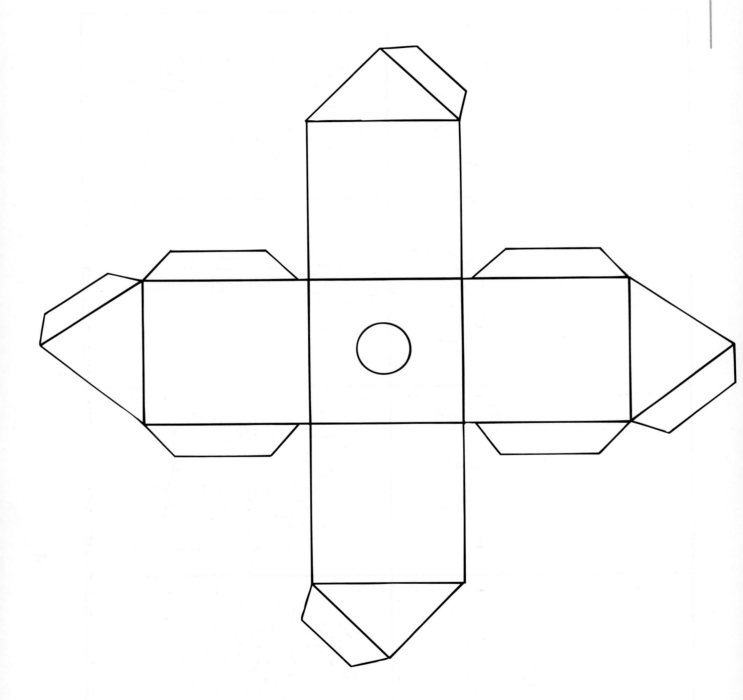

Dress the bear (1)

hat	coat
boots	jumper

Dress the bear (2)

scarf	dress
mittens	skirt
shirt	trousers
vest	socks

Tracks in the snow

'It's snowing!' said Dev, one morning as he woke up his brother, Kiran. The boys quickly got dressed and had their breakfast.

'Please, Mum, will you come and help us build a snowman in the field?' asked Kiran.

'Yes, of course, but put on your wellies, hats and coats first,' said Mrs Ahmed.

Soon the three of them were in the field behind their house.

'Let's make the snowman's body first,' said Kiran. He scooped up a big handful of snow off the floor and began to roll it into a ball. Dev helped to pat more snow onto the body. They soon had a large ball and began to roll it carefully along the ground.

As they got near the hedge, Dev shouted, 'Look what I've found! Monster tracks.'

'Let me see,' said Kiran.

On the ground were some footprints. The two middle toes were round. The toes at either side of the foot were egg-shaped. There were claw marks in front of each of the toes, and a big triangle at the back of the foot. Mrs Ahmed came over to find out what the boys were looking at.

'That looks like a fox footprint,' she said, 'we get foxes in the garden sometimes at night.'

'Let's see if we can find some more tracks,' shouted Dev as he ran over to some trees.

Kiran found some more footprints at the bottom of a tree. It looked as if some twigs had gone for a walk. Each print had three thin lines, like two Vs next to each other.

'I think that's a bird,' suggested Dev. 'Mum, come and see the bird tracks.'

'I've found some duck prints over here,' said Mrs Ahmed, 'I'll come and look at your footprints, and then you can see the ones that I've found by the pond.'

Mrs Ahmed thought that the bird prints could have been a robin's. The footprints she had found looked like the robin tracks, but there was a line in between each of the toes joining them together.

Kiran and Dev carefully looked at the bird tracks.

'They go right into the pond,' said Kiran.

'It might have been a duck.' Mrs Ahmed agreed with him.

'I can see lots and lots of big prints. They're the same size and shape as the bottom of my wellies,' said Dev, as he pointed at the ground. 'But I know exactly what made them – us!'

Lorraine Gale

Dear Father Christmas

20 Buttercup Road
Gristcaster
England

Dear Father Christmas

I really would like a new bike for Christmas, and a racing computer game. I also want a book about trains.

I know that the reindeers always find everybody's house each Christmas Eve but my mum helped me write some directions to get to our house, just in case the reindeers get lost.

I live in Buttercup Road. It is off Dandelion Road, on the left. There is a school at the end of the road. That is where Suzy, my sister, goes to school. She says that it's great. She likes reading and playing football.

In the middle of my road are a post office, a newspaper shop, and a greengrocer. I live on the same side of the road as the post office.

I live at number 20 Buttercup Road. There is a tree outside our house. On the right-hand side of the tree is a tall telegraph pole. We have a red gate. My uncle painted it the same colour as our front door last year.

I hope these instructions will help you to find my house.

Lots of love

Sean

Lorraine Gale